UNBLOCK ME

"The Journey of Mastering Your Life,
Overcoming Challenges,
and Embracing Your Worth"

BY

CHANTEL DENIESE

COPYRIGHT

Copyright © 2024 by: Chantel Denise Steinreich

All rights reserved. In accordance with the US Copyright Act of 1976, scanning, uploading and electronic sharing of any part of this book without the permission of the publisher is unlawful piracy and theft of the author's intellectual property. If you would like to use material from the book (other than for review purposes), prior written permission must be obtained by contacting the publisher at info@chanteldeniese.com

Library of Congress Control Number: TXu 2-424-938
Steinreich, Denise, Chantel, author. UNBLOCK ME "Mastering Your Life, Overcoming Challenges and Embracing Your Worth" Chantel D. Steinreich

ISBN: 979-8-9917584-0-6

Nitty Grit Books are available at special discounts for bulk purchases in the US by corporations, institutions and other organizations For more information, contact Nitty Grit Books at info@chanteldeniese.com

CONTENTS

INTRODUCTION i

CHAPTER ONE: IT HAPPENED TO ME 1

CHAPTER TWO: THE POWER OF CHOICE 13

CHAPTER THREE: UNBLOCK ME 21

CHAPTER FOUR: SELF-SOUL CARE 30

CHAPTER FIVE: HOPE HEALS 39

CHAPTER SIX: FORGIVENESS 49

CHAPTER SEVEN: UNDERSTANDING
YOUR WORTH 58

CHAPTER EIGHT: REMARKABLE YOU 71

CHAPTER NINE: NO REGRETS 78

CHAPTER TEN: OWN YOUR LIFE 86

CHAPTER ELEVEN: RHYTHM AND STRIDE 96

CHAPTER TWELVE: PRACTICE PURPOSE 103

REFERENCES 119

God,

*Thank you for your caring hands which have held me, healed me and guided me.
I am humbly grateful for your love.*

"For we are his workmanship, created in Christ Jesus for good works, which God prepared beforehand, that we should walk in them" (Ephesians 2:10)ESV

Acknowledgments

To my wonderful family John, Marie, Daphne, Melody, Aunt Gloria and Cousin T'kera—your love, support and encouragement means the world to me. I love you so much.

My amazing friends Shawn LaRe' Brinkley, Vicky McGhee, Lynn Brewer, and Dr. Daphne D. Burleson, your faithful friendship has brought me great joy.

Coach Jay Styles, thank you for walking me through the journey of writing my first book. Your expertise was invaluable.

There are many other contributors in my life who have blessed me. Thanks to all of you who have taught me a thing or two, prayed for me or shared a fresh word of inspiration. I want you all to know that I am extremely grateful for you.

INTRODUCTION

Growing up, I heard the saying, "Little girls are made of sugar and spice and everything nice." It was like a mantra. I remember saying it over and over and even singing it: "Sugar and spice and everything nice." If you are like me and are a part of the sweet tooth movement, then you know that a little sugar can be a girl's best friend. My palate enjoys every opportunity I can get to have a sweet fix.

As a young girl, I was told that I was very sweet. In that moment, I felt special and loved. But something happened when I got older. Those warm and loving comments from my younger years took a different turn into words that crushed my spirit. From my teenage years into my young adult years, I remember hearing words that did not align with what I had heard before, such as, "You are too difficult," "It's hard to love you," "Why can't you be like so and so?" "You never cease to amaze me," and "My last relationship was so much easier." OUCH! I never understood why people say such devastating and heartbreaking statements. The reality is that people will say cruel things and make their own interpretation of who you are, and some of us believe the negative comments they say. I did.

I personally believe that the "baby girl" years, for teens in particular, are the most defining moments in the life of a female. It's when you absorb everything you are told. This was when you faced things that you did not know what to do with, troubles that left you confused, rejections that made you question who you were, and all the other words and conversations that challenged your existence. For many of us, it's almost like a bad ghost that keeps coming to haunt us and follows us everywhere we go. It's as though the sugar has hardened and the spice is no longer preserving what once was. I love the "spice and everything nice" part of my childhood rhyme. Y'all know that spice is that good ingredient that makes food taste amazing. No one wants bland or yucky food, right? Enjoying your meal to satisfaction is something I think everybody wants. But that is not always the case, as there are times when it just doesn't taste right, and you don't like it.

Like our food, sometimes we don't like our lives. We often feel yucky about ourselves. There are many reasons why we feel this way. It could be because of the unpleasant things said to us. Perhaps we have encountered some form of trauma and haven't been able to cope with it. Or it could be that we haven't quite figured out how to make sense of our lives. Maybe little girls are not really made of sugar and spice and everything nice. Or perhaps they are. We will never know unless we take the journey of uncovering the truth about who we really are. The transitions of life are inevitable, but there is one thing we can all do, which is to equip ourselves with all we need to effectively live it well.

On my quest to figure out what little girls are made of, I discovered that there are different stages in life. They all are compositions of what I call "THE EXPERIENCE." Life is filled with many experiences, and we have the ability to learn and grow from them all.

It is extremely important for us to understand the power of our experiences. Our experiences do not define us, but they do affect who we are becoming. Roots are planted from our experiences, and they can either bless us or curse us. In the case of an experience, a blessing comes forth when a person chooses to view a difficult situation as an opportunity for something good. A curse, however, occurs when we only focus on the negative aspects of our experiences and let them lead us into bitterness. Unfortunately, many people choose the latter, even though it doesn't have to be this way.

One of the reasons I wrote this book is because I know that life brings many challenging experiences, but we all are capable of mastering them. Because we are worthy, there is so much potential for our past, present, and future to come together in harmony. We have the ability to soar in life. Each of us can prepare ourselves for the life ahead by declaring that the past does not get to control our present or future. Every one of us has access to this state of autonomy. If you have breath in your body, then there is more to experience, more opportunities to have, and a purpose for you to live out. We must never succumb to what was but instead always be striving for what is and what can be. Experiences are what life is all about, and we must embrace them in order to overcome, grow, and thrive.

Over the years, I have had to build a conviction that as a woman I can fully become my most powerful person—and you can too. I am a woman who believes in God, and I am convinced that He makes no mistakes. One of my favorite scriptures is Genesis 1:27. This scripture has blessed my life richly. It says, "So God created man in his own image, in the image of God he created him; male and female he created them." When I think of the word "image," I imagine likeness and resemblance. As I ponder this thought, I am humbly overwhelmed and excited for you and me. We are created by a Creator who designed us well. Therefore, it is our birthright to live wholeheartedly in the image in which we are created. This means that our next experience has the potential to be our best one yet.

Ladies, there is so much more to you, and although you are still developing, you are so ready to blossom. Words do not hold the power of who you are but instead are stepping stones to your purpose. We are all on a journey with different routes to pursue, but our experiences are gold mines ready for digging so that we can get to the gold. No one can love you more than how you need to love yourself. So, you must get intentional and do all that you can to experience every moment of loving yourself. Your mental, physical, emotional, and spiritual life deserves all of your attention, because your life was made on purpose, for purpose. It is time to embrace your "sugar and spice and everything nice" so that you can ignite your worthy life!

CHAPTER ONE

IT HAPPENED TO ME

*"Our experience is the catalyst
for shaping the best version of ourselves."*

Life can be so complicated! It happens from the time we wake up in the morning, to the daily tasks throughout the day, to that moment where you only hope for an ideal sweet spot called sleep that ultimately does not even come close to the amount we need. Then add all of the people we come in close contact with throughout our day: coworkers, friends, grocery store clerks, waiters, bankers, joggers, gym buddies, parents, spouses, children —and the list goes on. That alone can be overwhelming and messy. There were times when I got so frustrated with people that I wished I had a magic wand and could start making folks disappear. Don't judge, 'cause I know many of you have had this same wish.

As I've gotten older, my senses have become so alert. I am more aware of my own response in these interactions with humans and my personal need to live whole and complete. As humans, we are here to interact with other humans. It's the design of life. God made it this way. Unless you move to a deserted island where you are the only living being (which would be boring), then you are going to be around other skin-covered, heart-beating people. We actually need each other. Our lives are intertwined with other people's, and we would not be able to experience every stage of life without the ongoing interaction with others.

I mentioned "the Experience" in my introduction because it is a very important word that you will need to reflect on and refer to as you live your life. The process of any experience will either reveal something to you or grow you. Experiences are those things that we go through or create for ourselves. From the moment you were born into the world, you were officially birthed into an experience. Why do you think a baby cries when the doctor pops her bottom? It's because everything changed for her. She entered a world she did not know, and now she has to breathe on her own. Her life in the womb was her oasis. For nine months, she lived with what was familiar, consistent, and safe. Now she has to get accustomed to lights and different voices and sounds that are new to her. For the first time, she is seeing faces she has never seen before. That is a big experience for a tiny person. It happened to you and me. You didn't ask for this experience. It was your mommy and daddy who introduced you to your very first experience. The natural cycle of life just got real.

Life is filled with unlimited experiences. It's what becomes our greatest accomplishment or can be what we feel is the most debilitating moment of our lives. In the Merriam-Webster dictionary, experience is defined as a "practical contact with and observation of facts or events" or "the fact or state of having been affected by or gained knowledge through direct observation or participation." I like this definition because there are two parts to the experience. One is that which we are affected by, and the second is the knowledge we gain. This implies there is something to learn from it. If all human beings could adapt and adjust to these two simple words, "affected" and "knowledge," then we could soar beyond what we could imagine. These words can be a source of life-giving inspiration if applied well. I would even go on to say that it is very possible that if handled correctly, a person could actually have a better life and contribute to making the world more beautiful and brighter.

When I ponder the word "affected," it's very clear to me that something happened. Every person on the face of the earth has been affected in some way or another. When something affects us, we typically have a reaction to it. For example, if someone makes you mad, what do you typically do? Does your nice and calm attitude rise up, or do you retaliate? Or are you more comfortable with shutting down? Perhaps you ignore people, so you don't give them the time of day to intervene in your space. Maybe you are in denial and not in touch with your emotions. Most of us have gotten mad at some point in our lives; if you haven't yet, you will. Our responses may differ, but you will have one, and it could be either external or internal. Our experiences can leave us affected in various ways, and if we do not live in awareness of them, they will become the leader of our lives in everything we do. But there is also the other part of being affected that is good. Sometimes we have positive situations that affect us in a great way. And don't we all want those good times to roll in our lives? These kind of experiences are a huge win for us.

I spent many years reacting to the experiences in my life. I will never forget the time I placed as a runner-up in a beauty pageant. My spirits were flying high. It was an amazing experience. This was a big accomplishment for me. But when the excitement wore off and all the attention was gone, I felt empty. I made several attempts to secure my next exciting experience, so I entered another one. This time I did not place at all. In fact, the entire experience was a disaster. From uppity pageant directors to in-house discrimination, it left a bitter taste in my mouth. Then there were the "nice nasties": the girls who smile to your face but behind your back they talk about you like you were a dog. It was so ugly and just plain wrong. Does that make pageants a bad thing? Absolutely not! It's the experience that I had in the pageant, and it's on me to decide what I want to do with it.

Then there were other experiences, you know the ones, where you wish you could push the erase button and get rid of it. The ones that brought a lot of pain and tears. There have been times when I felt like my life was falling apart. I just wanted to delete what was happening. Our experiences are capable of having a hold on our life. So what do we do with them? What if we made every experience the ultimate experience by acknowledging, accepting, and adjusting to them? It would put us in the position of being a "manager" or, for a more catchy term, "boss." Managers and bosses are the leaders, decision-makers, and go-to people. With this kind of focus on your experiences, you can thrive in each one you encounter.

ACKNOWLEDGE

Taking the time to be present will strengthen your ability to connect with your experience. When you acknowledge something, you are embracing the existence or truth of it. There is so much wisdom and depth that can be gained from this perspective. Did you notice that this word has the root word "knowledge" in it? Hence, when you acknowledge a situation, you are gifted with knowledge. Girl, do you see where I am going with this?

Okay, so I need you to get completely involved. It is time to let these experiences know that you are fully aware of their presence and are prepared to face them. It is up to you to go toe-to-toe with your experiences. Acknowledging what happened and how you want to deal with it is very empowering. Knowledge is a life map, and acquiring it is foundational. Or you can ignore knowledge and live foolishly, making life a little bit harder for yourself. This will lead you to accumulate a heavy load of emotional suitcases. I have to tell you that handling it the second way will eventually wear you down. That's just too many bags to carry. Every experience will present a choice for you to make, and I encourage you to make your best one.

ACCESS

When we learn from what life has to offer us, we have access to approach life in a different way. Here is something that I had to come to terms with: we cannot determine the outcome of every experience, but we can examine our situation with curiosity and proceed accordingly. There are so many difficult situations, and it's easy to spend our energy on what happened. I want to do something right now that I have never done, which is to honor the amazing experiences in my life, because I have achieved some great things. On the flip side, I also want to respect my painful experiences.

Y'all, there is so much power in these two words. To honor and respect something is to show admiration and high regard. It is the equivalent of the way you will treat something or someone. I am not condoning having a high regard for my painful experiences. I would be lying to you if I told you that I admire those situations; however, I have accepted that they happened. I can't change them or go back in time to fix them. I will properly accept and respect the process of choosing my greatest growth in all my experiences. This is a great opportunity for you to do the same, because you get to be the "boss" and decide how you want to deal with your experiences.

ADJUST

There is always more to a story than what is presented, and making a few adjustments can help you in every area of your life. As individuals, learning, attaining, and discovering will lead us on a path of hope that elevates us into living authentically. When you make an adjustment, you are moving and changing something so that you get the desired condition or results you long for. It allows you to bring your situation into a better state. An example that comes to mind is a musician. Musicians are constantly adjusting their instruments. If a piano player is accompanying a singer, there may be a need for an adjustment. Maybe the key is too high and has to be lowered a whole step . This would be an adjustment that allows them to work in harmony as they create music together.

We all want to this kind of unity with ourselves. For many years, I wrestled with some things from my past that had me on lockdown mentally and emotionally. In many ways, I was stuck and unable to move forward in several areas of my life. When I decided to take a closer look at some of my experiences, that is when I flipped the script for my future.

Though I may not know you and may never get the opportunity to meet you, I want you to know that I am personally acknowledging that your experience exists for you and you are the only human being on this earth that has all of the details that affect you. This is your truth and your reality, and I do not make light of it, because I know this is your experience. I am in this with you all the way. I believe that you want to stand up and face your own situation because you are reading this book, which demonstrates that you want something better for yourself. That urge inside of you believes something is possible, and where there is belief, action must accompany it.

What would you like the next chapter of your life to look like? I guarantee you that whatever thought or picture that came into your mind, it is absolutely possible. If you want to see your possibility come to fruition, you will need to make an *investment* and a *commitment* to yourself. Take the time and commit to dealing with the experiences in your life. People who are willing and ready to do these two things can accomplish great things for themselves.

I decided to focus on my own experiences because I got tired of waking up feeling incomplete and looking at my life as if it were a mere slideshow for a presentation. I had learned how to play along with the events in my life, but I had not learned how to navigate the experience. When I was in the corporate world, I would show up for work and get it done because I was skilled at my job. The hours would go by fast, and I would soon find myself back at it again come 9:00 a.m. It was my routine. I am also an artist with over twenty-five years of performance history. I am passionate and excited every time I get to be on the stage or in front of a camera. These are some of my greatest experiences. They bring me a whole lot of joy.

When was the last time you acknowledged some of your own great experiences? Did you know that there is strength in thinking about the good things in your life? Another favorite scripture of mine is Philippians 4:8. It encourages me to think of great things. It says, "Whatever is true, whatever is honorable, whatever is just, whatever is pure, whatever is lovely, whatever is commendable, if there is any excellence, if there is anything worthy of praise, think about these things." Thinking of the great things in your life equips you for greatness. Greatness is what we can all attain if we choose it for ourselves.

What is one thing in your life that brought you happiness? It could be the dream job you got or when you went on your ideal vacation. What about when you graduated at the top of your class? How about when you opened your first business? Or remember when you finished high school, even though no one believed you would? Better yet, what about the fact that you have been through several heartbreaking relationships but you are still fighting the good fight? You got knocked down but got right back up and kept going. Take some time to entertain your reality. What was it like? What did you learn from it? How did it enhance your life? Get into the habit of finding the good times, because you will need them later. Every good experience that you have had can be a tool to help you with the new ones that will come. So let the good stuff sink in and be blessed by what has already gone well.

Your life is a God-given gift that you get to unwrap every day. Take the time to be present and enjoy your experiences. What do you think it would look like if you did not have anything else to do other than to take care of yourself? Allow yourself to picture this. What do you see? I know it may be hard for some of you, because many of you are busybodies taking care of the entire world. You are the movers and groovers, shakers and bakers. Things get done on your watch, and that is a good thing. But the truth is, one must never spend all of their goodness scattered in so many places and neglect their own soul. Our soul is counting on us to feed it well. The world has been managing itself way before you were born, so it's okay to take a break, because we all need one.

It's time to pivot and build better habits for yourself. According to Merriam-Webster, a habit is "an acquired mode of behavior that has become nearly or completely involuntary or a pattern acquired by frequent repetition." This is exactly what you will need to create consistency in order to blossom in all your experiences. Here is a habit that I have found to be constructive: the process of writing down affirmations that help you turn your experiences into everyday life tools. So, let's get to it. Grab a Post-it note or your journal and write down one word that comes to your mind. Don't take too much time with this. Let the word come to you. It could be one that you have heard before. It may be one that brings a smile to your face.

One of my favorite words is "peace." My life hasn't always been peaceful, but, girl, I have claimed this for myself. I keep this word with me wherever I go. When the winds of life blow a little hard and I can't quite navigate the challenges, I pray for peace. And I have to tell you that every time I do, I feel the calm. I don't know about you, but I need my peace. Peace gives me the freedom to not have to figure out why something happened. It helps me go through the process without feeling the need to fix or solve my problem.

The experiences in our lives alone can drain our good energy, leaving us depleted. So we need to replenish ourselves by doing and creating things that fill us up. You can start by imagining small ways to overcome any challenging experience. One thing that comes to mind is running a race. When a person wants to run a marathon, they do not wait until the day of the race to prepare for it. Each step they take and every move they make prior to the race prepares them for the bigger event. They make small steps toward their goal, knowing that the big step is the actual race. Starting small is a form of preparation that ultimately grants you bigger steps to take in the long run. Your experience will not wait for you to prepare yourself. It is the small steps that will help you make your next best move. When you take this approach, it will keep you from putting all your energy and efforts into something that may only need a super simple solution to deal with it.

There is a story about David and Goliath in the Bible that I love, which may help shed some light on this concept. If you don't know it, it's one that will surely inspire you. Goliath was this giant guy, and David was a young sheepherder. He was a smaller guy compared to Goliath. Goliath came out all puffed up to fight David. David came forth with a slingshot and five smooth stones. Well, the story didn't end well for Goliath. David used one stone and knocked Goliath out with one pull from his sling. The moral of this story is that you can use what you have to face any obstacle in life. A small habit will give you the upper hand over every experience. How we have dealt with our experiences in the past may require us to use a different approach for future ones.

Lastly, there are two fundamental things that I have discovered over the past three years that have paved the way for a new direction for myself: mindset and worth. It is my responsibility to manage my own mind and live in my own worth. They are inseparable for me. How I do this is through the practice of a PARADIGM SHIFT, which, by the way, is one of my habits. It is defined as "an important change that happens when the usual way of thinking about or doing something is replaced by a new and different way." Example: In a difficult situation, I often focus on finding some good in it. I use the good as a reminder of who I am and what I am trying to accomplish. I also choose not to let what is hard dictate the outcome of my day. Now I think through my experiences from a place of knowing my worth. Before this, the experience happened, and it left me with no hope of where to place it. Where there is no hope, the experiences pile up, and before you know it, there is an enormous feeling of overwhelming defeat. If David had looked at his experience with Goliath through the lens of what was obvious, he would have been overtaken by the experience. He used what he had and thought differently about his situation.

Experiences come in all shapes and forms. It is mandatory that we develop habits, practices, and standards that prepare and equip us for our interactions with the experience. Living your life in this way is one of the best things you can do for yourself.

You are worth it, and you are so ready for this. Allow yourself to expand your mind and extend your heart to something different. Believe and achieve all at the same time. You can do it!

CHAPTER TWO

THE POWER OF CHOICE

"Life is like a box of chocolates."
Forrest Gump

Have you ever seen the movie *Forrest Gump*? If you have, you know the defining moment when Forrest says, "Life is like a box of chocolates." I absolutely loved that line in the movie, but in my real life, I was like, *What the heck is he talking about? How can he compare life to chocolate? Does he know what I have been through?* Or better yet, *Does he know what* we *have been through?* There is so much that goes in opposition to this statement. Life does not work this way. We go through real-life situations, and it is far from being as good as chocolate is to me.

Forrest had a challenging situation. Life was not perfect, but his mindset was one where he saw potential, and this is why he could compare life to chocolate. But how can we apply this to our own lives? Y'all know that a box of chocolate can have a variety of flavors or be all the same. Are you the girl who likes everything the same, or do you like a little variety? The good thing is that if it's the same, you know what you are getting. And if it's your favorite, you are a happy girl. On the other hand, variety can be a challenge because you don't know what you are getting, so you have to take your chances. You may have to sample a few of them till you get to the one you like. Can you imagine if we approached life this way? Sampling everything! This could either be a win, or we might become "samplers" who can never find satisfaction. And having everything the same over and over again can become mundane. Personally, I like variety, because it allows me to have options and find what I like.

Now, here's the scoop: there is nothing wrong with what you like. The challenge is trying to have things go your way all the time. Life doesn't always align the way we want it. This is a hard truth for those of us that like to be in control. Being in control is really only a form of pseudo-control. The truth is, the only thing we all have control over is our choices, and life is filled with many of them. So having a variety of options may work in our favor. We get to choose what we will do with the options that are offered to us. Forrest Gump wasn't fixated on his circumstance. He took a piece of chocolate and made a declaration for himself. How does somebody do that when life has been so difficult?

Some of you have experienced challenge after challenge, and even as you are reading this, you are facing one right now. It feels like you can't get a break. You're exhausted and weary, because it's wearing you down. I have experienced all of the above. You are not alone. For years, my life was a heavy load. I carried all my burdens everywhere I went. It was like going up a hill with a sofa on my back. Each step upward got harder and harder. Though I kept making efforts to move forward, I could never get to the top. Have you ever felt that way? Feeling like you can't take another step because you don't know where it will lead you? Back then, I discovered that I had a lot of blocks in my life. The pain of my past held me hostage.

As a young girl, I was abused sexually, physically, and mentally. Where I grew up, I believe this type of abuse was happening often, but it was not something that anyone ever mentioned. My friends were experiencing it, but they'd better not even think to talk about it because it could stir up trouble in the town. One of the predators in my situation told me that if I told anyone, he would kill my baby brother. Well, I was about nine and a half years old at the time, and at that age most of us believe what we are told. So, for two years I didn't say a word. Until one day I said, "NO more!" I decided to take my chances and stand up for myself for the first time. I called my mom on the phone, and she rushed home from work. I also had a friend who was a witness because she was there. We were both victims. The cops got involved, and before I knew it, there was a case and a hearing date. Since I was so young, they would not let me speak at the court hearing. To make matters more difficult, the other girl's family decided they did not want to pursue legal charges, which meant I would be on my own. They withdrew her story and said that she made it up.

I can't tell you why they chose to lie. But what I will say is that when truth is suppressed, many people suffer. The judge decided that I had probably made it up as well, so they dismissed the case. Though my family believed me, there was nothing they could do about that decision. To this day, I feel that it was unfair; I never received justice. The predator was left to prey on their next victim.

But what about me? I felt strange and ashamed all at the same time. I moved away for two years to go live in the big city in Houston, Texas. There I thought I would have the freedom to get away from what happened—but instead I found myself caught up in acting out from my emotional and mental suffering. I was in a lot of pain. You see, pain is potent, and it will have a hold on you if you don't get the proper help to work through it. I did not get the help that I needed for a very long time. I hid my pain and tucked it away so that no one could see it—or so I thought.

Y'all, there are so many forms of pain, and it is happening all over the world. There are a lot of people hurting everywhere. You may be in some kind of pain. We cannot escape this unending thing that happens to all of us, and we cannot diminish its presence. I know that this is a touchy topic. It's painful just thinking about it. You may not be ready to deal with it, and that is okay. I hope and pray the work this book offers will be beneficial for you and will give you some tender, comforting, and strengthening life tools to assist you. I will ask you many questions throughout these chapters. The goal is to help you learn how to get in front of your pain and take a chance on you. You can do this, and you can do it well.

I wish I had known then what I know now. It is my desire to pay it forward and share as much with you as I can about what I have learned over the years—in particular, how I make great choices that help me live a full, healthy life, even in painful and difficult situations.

First, let's start with a very important thing that we all

must take notice of when it comes to understanding the pain in our lives. Pain has many indicators that show up. These indicators, when ignored, can often deceive us and undermine the choices we make in life. So therefore, we must recognize them and choose how we will deal with them.

THE INDICATORS

There are several indicators that reveal a person is in pain. Indicators of pain come in different forms, such as anger, resentment, irresponsible behavior, extreme reactions, irritability, inability to take responsibility, depression, sadness, and the like. For example, when a person reacts to everyone and everything around them from a place of defense, usually they are experiencing some kind of pain. Defenses can be good in a sport or when you have to stand up for yourself. However, if you are functioning defensively in every area of your life, it's a problem because it robs you of your inner peace. To react to everyone as if they are attacking you sucks up all of your good energy and will leave you spiritually dehydrated. This can be pretty exhausting.

As I was writing these words, my body got stiff, because I remembered all the times I gave over my peace only to become a prisoner of my own pain. Because of my response to my pain, I would go around looking for the next criminal that I could personally prosecute. I would create stories in my head where I would literally think that my friends might harm my children. My mind was full of scenarios and suspicion that I created. I struggled to have healthy male relationships. Every man that came in my space had to prove their innocence in my life. I kept repeating this scene, and I must say that there was never a good ending to the story. Unfortunately, this was a pattern I lived in for a very long time.

Maybe you see some similarities. If there is any undealt with pain in your life, it will reveal itself. Pain also makes plans to protect self, and it fights with everyone else. We don't have to live through this kind of cycle. It will continue until you examine every area of your life and release what is no longer needed for your path. If you have been abused like I was or in any other way, I want to acknowledge it and tell you that my heart is saddened about all that you have been through. I know it's hard. It was hard for me. I want to offer you this hope: there is more on the other side of your pain. You can be victorious. But you will need to make yourself completely available and aware of the details of your pain so that you can identify every moment that needs your care.

A good way to get in touch with this is by asking questions that will stir up a conversation with yourself about it. Is there any pain in your life? How do you deal with it? Is it taking up space deep inside your heart? What choices have you made about it?

What I am about to say may be difficult, but allow yourself the opportunity to embrace what happened. What I mean is connect all of you with your pain. Don't ignore it or resist it, because if you do, it will keep you from the growth that is ahead. Sis, this is a green light moment that I want you to make a move on. You get to assert your power of choice in everything that has happened to you.

Here are three concepts about the ability to choose. May they spark joy in you as you read them.

- CHOICE EMPOWERS – You are in the position of authority, giving you the confidence you need that builds courage to face anything.
- CHOICE INVIGORATES – Your choice gives you the strength and energy you need to undertake any situation that comes your way. It's a lifeline!
- CHOICE TRANSFORMS – It allows the kind of change you want in your life. It builds your character and illuminates your inward and outward presence.

Your pain does not get to rule over you if you choose to be the leader over it. Nor does the person who hurt you get to have power over your life. You are the only one who has the choice to give them permission to have that kind of access. So don't do it. Let your choices be of service to you. Asserting your choice allows you the ability to experience change in your situation. This also will help you have some peace in your soul. It doesn't mean that you will not remember what happened to you. This is a process that will lead you to become an overcomer. I had to come face-to-face with my own stuff, and so do you. It is a choice that you get to choose for yourself, and it is a gifting of goodness into your own life. So, don't ever settle for scraps or pieces of you. You deserve all of you.

Additionally, there is another action step that I took when I started working through my past pain, which was to talk about it. Communication is such a great and effective tool that actually benefits us and those we share our stories with. It's the best method to teach someone about who you are. An online resource called "Skills You

Need" says, "Being able to communicate effectively is perhaps the most important of all life skills." It is what enables us to pass information to other people.

When was the last time you talked about your pain? For over fifteen years, I did not tell anyone what had happened to me. It was buried so deep that I had to spend months of what felt like digging up a grave to get to the bottom of it all. In the 90s, I moved to Los Angeles and started attending a church. For the first time, I was able to share my story with a group of women who had been through something similar. We didn't compare, cover up, or dismiss our experiences. We acknowledged and grieved them. Then we chose our future journey. Sometimes just uttering the words of your wound is key to living the life you want.

Do you have someone in your life that knows your story? Is there someone you feel safe with? Have you been in any groups like the one I mentioned? Is your support system strong? If none of this is in order for you, you can work on building this area of your life today.

Everything we do in life will require us to make a choice. That power lies within your hands. I want to challenge you to go all the way for you so that you can discover that "life is like a box of chocolates," and so much variety awaits you. You get to decide your what, when, and how, so make your best choice.

CHAPTER THREE

UNBLOCK ME

"We are becoming who we have chosen to be."

Do you remember when you were a teenager? Those teenage years can be fickle. All of the competition, trying to fit in, discovering who you are, and the excitement of boys. Dealing with puberty, pimples, and so on. Our hormones are in overdrive.

Pediatricians say that kids are impressionable up to five years of age, when their personality becomes fully intact. They are already playing grownup at this age. For me, this was true, because both of my girls revealed themselves to me at that age, and I could clearly see who they were becoming. As the years passed and we approached their teenage years, it was then that I realized their experiences were making and shaping their character.

Let me tell you what I learned about teenagers. They are smart but do silly things. They are brilliant but can become bitter. They are loving but can often live lazy. They are the future, but some choose failure. They are leaders but can be led astray. At this age there is so much potential, but there are so many distractions and a lot of growing pains. What happens in the teenage years often shadows our years ahead. Many of us carry our teenage years into our adult life. I know this because some of us are still talking about what happened to us then. However, for some, it's your testimony, and you share the experience to help others. Then there are many of us who are anchored in the pain of our past. We are living in an adult body but under teenage management. It's from this perspective that we manage all of our emotions and make our decisions. Rather than responding to life, we are reactors to everything and let our feelings be our guide.

Despite all this, there is a myth that I want to challenge: being a teenager is not the worst stage of life. I remember when I shared some of my challenges as a parent. Most people would ask, "How old are your kids?" At that time, I had a teen and a preteen. When I shared this information, people would immediately respond, saying, "Those are the worst years!" Think about that for a second. If these are the worst years, then what's next? Is it going to get better? Back then, I wasn't even considering what could get better. All of my attention was focused on the worst. And needless to say, I accepted those comments. But this is so not true. Y'all, if we see the teenage years as the worst, that's what we will experience. For those of us who are parents, we have to dismiss the negative programming about our teens. I'm saying this stuff because I absolutely 100 percent saw the worst in my kids. I saw every mistake, flaw, and imperfection, and let me tell you, both girls felt it all even without me ever saying a word. Our energy is a great communicator of what we feel and think about others and ourselves.

Something that really helped me understand the world of a teenager was reminding myself that they are humans discovering life. Their peers are the ones whom they trust and that make them feel special. They often think their parents don't understand them like their friends do. They think we are out of the times, so it can be hard for them to share their life with their parents. I get it. There is one thing that we have in common with teens, and that it is acknowledging we all were a teen at some point in our lives. I do not believe that the teenage years are the worst years. These are the foundational years of becoming. And this is a continuing process toward who we are today. We are becoming the person we have chosen to be. The teenage years are often where many of us need to go back to in order to discover more about ourselves.

As a teenager, I was very secretive. I stayed in my own head and heart most of the time. I grew up in the late 80s, and I must say, though the years have passed and I have seen a few decades go by, anatomy is still consistent. Teens today are still dealing with some of the same things that I dealt with during my teenage years, like seeking approval from others and trying to fit in or being liked. They are having to learn how to navigate life just like we did. In fact, due to the condition of our world today, teens are facing more life difficulties and more trauma than previous generations. It's all quite over-whelming. Young minds are having to grow into adult minds really fast. The truth is that we are more alike than not. Life does not come without a few hard knocks. But those hard knocks can be like soil that fertilizes growth when properly rooted. And don't we all want to mature beyond our teenage years?

No one wants to be stagnant, but very often we find ourselves in this place. Unfulfilled dreams, hopeless habits, diluted thoughts, diminished desires, and a lack of vision have become our closest companions. We hold onto things that do not work for us anymore. Why do we do this to ourselves? Perhaps it is because we've listened to what others said about us as a teenager. Maybe it is because we have unresolved pain to deal with. Or could it be that we just don't truly believe we have what it takes to do something great with our lives? If this is your narrative, what evidence do you have to support it? Some of us have entertained so many false accusations that they have become a part of the story we tell ourselves daily. It is time for us to stop living in this painful place. Every lie you tell yourself blocks the potential opportunities you have. The mind tells every part of your body what to do because the brain is the control center. Therefore, you must retrain your brain.

When I moved to California, I decided to make some changes. I wanted to make a better future for myself. I did not want the stuff that happened to me to be my forever. I was not interested in having my past be my roommate. I wanted a fresh new start. Fresh starts are so good, y'all, because they give you a new opportunity. My idea of a fresh start is to focus on what it is that blocks you so that you can get unblocked. This can be a challenge when trying to overcome the barriers and blocks in your life but absolutely possible. It starts with reevaluating your life in ways that your mind can visualize newness for yourself.

I had to consider my ways: How I talked to people. My mood on a daily basis. If I had joy or not. There were a few things to examine, even though I was scared of what I might discover. I had to ask myself the right questions, and you can do the same thing too. Ask yourself questions that lead to what you want out of life. Examples: "Is this my best offering of myself?" "Does what I am thinking line up with what I want?" "What is holding me back in my life?" "When I go to sleep at night, do I feel good about myself?" "Do I sleep well?" "Am I still holding onto old wounds?" "What happened to me?" The last one is usually that defining moment. It is fully packed with the pieces to your puzzle. The answers to these questions can unleash the beginning steps toward creating change for you and also helping those around you.

I didn't know that I was blocked. When I decided to approach my life in my newness, I started studying the Bible. I went to church most of my teenage years, but I was brand-new when it came to digging into the scriptures. My first attempt was difficult, because I wasn't ready. I had a million excuses and would push this process to the side. However, when you know deep down inside you need help, you will eventually seek it and get it. After a couple of years of avoiding the bible, I decided to try and study it again. This was the right time for me and I began to learn new things from the scriptures that enhanced my life. I got to learn about Jesus and how he dealt with life and it's difficulties. When I took inventory of my life, I noticed how negative I had been. I also noticed my unhelpful habits. For example, if I was not happy in a relationship, I treated the person like he/she was disposable. I also did not take advice from anyone. I had not allowed others to get too close to me for fear of being hurt again.

Y'all, I wasn't raised this way. I *chose* this way. It was easier to operate from this place. How does a person who was not trained this way become this way? It's because of the shaping and molding that takes place throughout our lives as we live on this earth. As a result, we need to learn a new way of dealing with our life experiences. I had not developed any tools during my teenage years that would help me in my young adult life. I was only able to see my potential after I learned some life-transforming directives from the Bible. But even then, it would take me twenty years to fully embrace it, and at the age of forty, I found myself begging God to "UNBLOCK ME." It was then that I paid attention to how Jesus did not let what happened to him rule him.

I started retraining my mind to think differently about my situation so that I could live the life I wanted. Though it was hard, I was excited to do a new thing. When I reviewed my life, it was very clear that I had been operating from my past pain. It had infiltrated deep into my core. I looked at what it had done to me and how it had shaped me. I was determined to win in my circumstances, and I believe that everyone who wants a real shot at life will do the same. It took faith for me to embrace the scriptures, just like it would require faith for me to do this kind of life work. In John 16:33, Jesus said, "In the world you will have tribulation. But take heart! I have overcome the world." This has become another one of my favorite scriptures because it prepares me. I will have experiences that are difficult, but my Lord has overcome it. Because of this, I too can be an overcomer. When I set my mind to overcoming, everything became possible. To this day, the Bible is my go-to for positive thinking and living.

The experiences we have will affect our thought process, and the actions we take need reflection. The reality of shaping is that it takes place by either imagination or representation. Clay is a great example of this. The reason kids like it so much is because they can let their creativity run wild and make all kind of shapes with it. This is the same process that we experience as adults. As we grow from a child to an adult, our shape changes. We are being shaped into a form that we either love or do not love. We can't change much about our physical growth process, but we sure can change the inward parts, like our mind, heart, and spirit.

If you want to give it your all and be a living change in this world, getting unblocked means you are going to have to get up close and personal with your life. One thing that will help you is to be aware of the LIFE BUSTERS (LBs) that are crushing you. Life Busters are things that attempt to interrupt or destroy all of the best in you. They are tricky and will intervene daily. Let me give you a few to evaluate: false narratives, self-doubt, self-sabotage, self-discrimination, faithlessness, cynicism, bad company, abuse of any kind, lack of hope, avoidance or ignoring, tolerations, unhealthy intake, absorbing others, and anything that is a sister or brother to any of these. If you are nurturing any of these, know that they are keeping you from the life you want. These LBs come to wreak havoc on your soul.

Recognizing who you do not want to be gives you room to become who you *do* want to be. I know you don't want to be mean, spiteful, hateful, nasty, and angry. Chile, nah! You did not wake up with these goals in mind. If you are experiencing any of this, it's something you chose, but it is not what you would have written down on a piece of paper expressing that you want to live your life like this. So, what are you going to do about it?

How long will you let these Life Busters take residence in your life? You have to put them in their place, because they do not belong in that great big heart of yours.

I will be honest and tell you that doing this life work is a difficult process. I have to speak this truth, because if I faked the facts, I would be wasting your time—and I am not about to do that. But because I care and am committed to the community of sisterhood, I'm coming to you with what I know to be true. With that said, you are in good company. It's not going to be easy, but it is better to live forward than exist with no movement. Things happen to us and for us. Either way, it shapes the way we think and how we do life.

So what Life Buster is it for you? Acknowledge it, but do not for one second be ashamed of it. Shame does not produce anything. The goal is change, not shame. The changes you make will remind you of the grit you have inside you.

Take it a step further and declare your destiny. Grab a mirror right now. Look into it and say your name out loud. Do this three times. After that, tell yourself one thing that you will no longer do, and then one new thing you will do for yourself. It could go something like, "I will no longer live as a procrastinator," or "I will finish college and get my degree." Or get radical, such as, "Today, I am going to get rid of all the clothes that I can no longer wear."

I do realize that some of us have some deep stuff to unblock, and I want to acknowledge that. This is not in any way a cure or remedy for your situation. This is simply a tool that will help as you take steps toward your greater good. Because life is all about growing up and showing up, you deserve to step up in this world with every part of who you are. It's taking on the shaping years and moving into the molding process toward "solidification." In human form, it's being solid on who you want to be and humble enough to know that you must continue to grow.

Lastly, I want to leave you with this concept that I hope will empower your mind. It is simple but has a wonderful metaphor attached to it. Think about a banana. When it's green, it is in the development stage. It's not ripe for eating. When it turns yellow, everyone knows that it is ready for enjoying, but before we can take our first bite, we have to unpeel it. It is the same with us. The unblocking process is like the unpeeling of a banana. So, I want to encourage you to be okay with this step in your life. It's necessary for us all to allow ourselves the experience of going through the development and ripening stage. And in time, you will enjoy the fruit of your life as you unpeel every layer.

CHAPTER FOUR

SELF-SOUL CARE

"Bask in the warmth of your own light."
Amy Perez

Did you know that self-care starts with identifying your need for it? It's about being curious about the opportunities self-care offers and knowing your body well enough to know when it needs servicing. It's like any other need in life. You wouldn't let your refrigerator leak water and ignore it, because then you'd have a big mess all over your kitchen floor. So, to avoid all of that, you would repair it. It's the same way with your body. It's in constant need of care. And when it is not taken care of, things start falling apart and life gets messy. But when we are in touch with our bodies, we make self-care happen. We may go to the spa, get a massage or our nails done, have glamour time with hair and makeup appointments, and the list goes on. Often there is a lot of attention to the outward parts of our body for self-care. And you will get no complaints from me, because I love a good self-care day. However, our body has inner and outer parts that both need our conscious care and attention.

Many women spend more time on their outer beauty and neglect their inner care. Why do you think this is? Perhaps it's easier to do the outward care. Inner care is a much longer process. Inner care has many levels, and it can be an overwhelming journey. The truth is that we need inner care just as much, because it allows us to take care of our soul. In order to experience wholeness, we as women must evaluate and investigate our options for "self-soul care." People who are intentional about their inner care are some of the most influential people on the planet. They are on a mission for total wellness, and so they live it. Self-soul care is a main component of the human existence, which involves the mind, body, soul, and spirit.

Self-care groups have been around for a long time. They're part of the process of establishing behaviors to ensure holistic well-being for yourself. These support systems of self-care have a huge impact on us all. Men and women both benefit from the resources that are available. But what happens when there are no groups or friends asking you questions like: "Are you okay? Is there anything I can do for you?" Or how about challenging you to take care of your heart because it's beating outside your body? Sometimes folks will watch you behave a certain kinda way and just ignore it. Maybe they are scared of the conflict that might arise if they spoke to you about your situation. It's possible that those who are close to you will check in on you, but many people do not have friends like this. In many situations, some find themselves alone trying to figure out how to cope with the life they have. This is why it is important to learn yourself better than anyone else. In all honesty, our life is our responsibility. We don't ever need to wait for someone to check in on us. We must check in on ourselves. Our good friends don't need to bail us out of every situation when we have the ability to take care of ourselves.

As I watch the trend of social media and ongoing quarrels, I have witnessed the crises of bleeding hearts. So many people are frustrated with life, and only a few realize their own pain. Their practice of freedom of speech is the spillover, and many of them have no one in their life who will actually help. One of the saddest things to watch is another person's life fall apart in front of you. Nowadays people record these moments and post them on social media platforms, not to educate but to humiliate. I am sure you have seen it. Folks making fun of other people's emotional breakdowns. What they don't realize is that the moment they are watching comes from years of unresolved or current pain. Y'all, these episodes are not to be ignored. They are serious situations and they indicate a person's need of self-soul care. Wellness must become a priority. So this means, as individuals, we need to be aware when we are at our capacity and in need of self-soul care.

Self-soul care is the concept of helping ourselves in action. It's actually one thing we do have control of. Did you know that every organ in your body is supported by another organ? If one part is suffering, eventually another part will join in by default. It's the natural order of things, which supports the need to take care of all of you. It is very important to understand that the deeper you go, the more you will be in tune with yourself.

In reality, self-care is soul-care. When you think about it, the soul needs nourishment just like the skin. Our soul is the part of us that involves our mind and emotions. It is the immaterial part of a human being that can respond to others. It gives us the ability to relate to each other and form bonds. The inner parts of you will always show up whether you take care of the outer parts of you or not. You will not be able to cover up this part of you for long. Eventually it will burst forth without your permission. That is why it has to be at the top of the list if you want to become the best version of yourself. So, girl, let's do the work!

Understand that everyone who wants a life that they honor must have faith that it is possible. Mindset is everything when it comes to building a healthy life. Previously, I mentioned that there are different forms of pain and each one must be identified. I like to categorize them into four different areas: physical, mental, emotional, and spiritual. All of these can be intertwined, but one is usually the primary one. I know that many of you may have physical pain from an injury or illness. I will not be discussing the how-to for this type of pain. It is better for you to consult with a professional for this kind of pain. I will also make a statement for anyone who may have some deeper emotional pain that is in need of psychological care that you pursue it for yourself if need be. I am not a psychologist or therapist, and the information in this book is not designed to be a replace-ment. There are many professionals in these fields. They are the experts, so let them assist you if you need it. My desire is to share tools that I have personally learned and have had great success with in dealing with pain in hopes that they will benefit you too.

The goal for this exercise is to focus on nurturing the inner parts of your body. I recommend choosing only one area of pain to start with. It is impossible to deal with several areas of pain all at the same time. Don't do this to yourself, because it could potentially disrupt your progress.

In order to deal with some of our past or present pain, we first need to get clear on what it is that continues to disturb our soul. The very first thing I want to let you know is that you will need to make time for this process. When I started writing this book, my coach told me that I would have to set aside the time and prioritize it like any other appointment I was committed to. He was calling me to excellence in my life, and I appreciated it. With that said, I have to pass the baton to you and call you to do the same, because your life is so valuable, and it needs your full participation.

I want to you to take a moment to pause and think about what day of the week you could dedicate time to focus on yourself. Next, decide what time works for you and how long. And, lastly, decide where you will do this. Wherever you choose, make sure it is quiet and that there will be no possible interruptions. This will get you started. After you have made your decision, put it on your calendar. Now you have officially made a commitment to yourself. Way to go!

Here is what you are going to need for your self-soul care day: a journal, a box of tissues, and some water. On the day that you have chosen for yourself, take these three items, go to your space, and begin. On the very first page of your journal, write down what you believe is an area of pain in your life. This may not come forth right away, but sit still with it. This is a perfect opportunity for you to get down on your knees, pray, meditate, and ask God for guidance. Whatever time you have allotted for this, do not cut it short because you can't think of anything in the moment. Keep sitting until you can recall a moment. Then, underneath that, write down what emotions, feelings, or reactions you are having about it. The reason this is very necessary is because it allows you the opportunity to get close and personal with your experiences. Get excited because you have officially started your empowering process.

There are various clues that you can use to investigate your situation. I have listed a few below.

- Fear
- Anger
- Shame
- Sadness
- Grief
- Depression
- Stress
- Frustration
- Isolation
- Negative thoughts
- Loneliness
- Feelings of worthlessness

Are you experiencing any of these? If you are feeling angry, it's very possible that someone hurt you in some way. If you are grieving, you may have lost someone you love or something you valued. Loneliness can be an indication of abandonment. There are many other clues, and the specific one for you may not be listed. With that said, try to find one that may be helpful for you. This exercise is like giving your pain a name.

Okay, I have to confess that I chose several of the above clues, but then I had to go back because it's better to start with just one. Once I narrowed it down, "feelings of worthlessness" was staring me in the face. These feelings are strong forces within. Why do we feel these emotions so powerfully? It's because something took place inside of us, and we must attend to it. Ignoring it will not make it go away. Trust me! When we ignore pain, we are only suppressing the truth of what happened or what is happening.

Another thing I want you to understand is that none of these pain clues indicate areas of your life that you need to be embarrassed about. Embarrassment is a life imposter, because it deceives you. It focuses on making you feel ashamed and keeps you stuck so that you will not tell anyone. You need to stand up to it and choose you. And as you do so, you will strengthen your awareness of anything that attempts to mislead you. Pay attention to what stands out for you during this process. Make sure you write it down. Be very specific. Something did happen, and it affected you. But even though it happened, it is not supposed to take up residence in your life. If it is not paying you rent, it needs to be gone. What we believe about what happened to us is where we need to spend dedicated time. We can't change what happened to us, but we can change the trajectory of what we will do with what happened to us.

Some of you may feel like it was your fault. And I am here to tell you that is false and is one of the biggest lies that seeks to disturb your soul. There is good and there is evil. We don't make people do things to us. They do it because, somewhere deep down inside, they are off.

Off-center, off target, off the radar of God's goodness. They chose to do what they did. No one made them. And the same goes for all of us. No one makes us do anything. I will say this loudly again with passion! Choice is our most powerful possession. So don't give anyone your power. And don't take responsibility for someone else's wrong choice that affected you.

When we are reacting to folks or going off on them because we are mad, we are creating more trouble for ourselves. The enemy who I am going to name is Satan. His strategy is to have you so wrapped up in your pain that you start pouring it out on others. If all of us end up fighting and hurting each other, there will be no room for healing or hope. Pain will claim its fame while the world watches. Who wants to stare at pain all day long? Not me!

Identifying the real issue is the assignment. I know you don't want your identity to be represented by your pain, but your investigation process is crucial. What happened to you is not your responsibility, but it is your responsibility to self-soul care your situation. When I realized that my own pain was building a fire in other areas of my life, I decided to put the flame out.

I used to feel sorry for myself and complain about how my life wasn't going the way that it should. I felt like I had missed my window of opportunity to fulfill my dreams. My fear, anger, and a lack of worthiness were obvious, and I knew in my heart that God was calling me to get real so that I could heal. There is so much God has in store for people like you and me, so we don't have time to nurse old wounds or pacify past experiences. Life is too short for that kind of living.

We all must come to a place of reality and reflection in order to move forward. This kind of attention to self is much needed, and the reward is even greater. So instead of letting your feelings loose in the grocery store, on social media, or even during a personal road rage tour, be free to pour all of you out into the pages of your journal in a quiet place where only you can hear what is going on inside you. Allow yourself these sweet moments of intentional self-soul care. You can also do exercises that will calm your soul and enhance your experience, such as meditation, listening to nature sounds, or focusing on the sound of the water when you take a shower. For more ideas, *HuffPost* has twelve amazing exercises, which are listed in my references.

Self-soul care is a hopeful practice which can enable the light of your soul to shine brightly. Your story is still being written, and if you make taking care of you a priority, you will watch the story of your life blossom and unfold into a beautiful movie that you long to see.

CHAPTER FIVE

HOPE HEALS

"I feel that my story is my legacy, and I have to pass it on."
Tina Turner

One of my daughters came to me one day and told me that she did not like the scars on her face. She had developed sores all over her face, which left several blemishes on her skin. I understood the difficulty she was having, but I did not acknowledge the pain she was experiencing. We went to several doctors year after year trying to find out what this unusual kind of sore was. The doctors diagnosed her with a bad case of eczema. They gave us all kinds of different creams to use, but none of them healed the sores. I began to question the doctors' credibility, because I did not think they knew what they were talking about. I knew what eczema looked like, and her case did not look like it to me.

Finally, I decided to go to a homeopathic doctor because I just knew it was something bigger. Upon the first visit, he told us it was eczema. I was like, "Are you serious?" He said, "Yes." Then he proceeded to show me the different kinds of eczema from his book of pictures.

I had never seen so many severe cases before. The doctor educated me about the kinds and stages of eczema people experience. My daughter had a really intense case that left her scarred. He gave her some herbal medication, and it healed and closed up the wounds—but the scars were still there. He also told me that her scars could diminish a bit, but it would take time. I would have to try another product, which was rather costly. I knew that I did not have the money to do so.

I am saddened to say that I did not follow through on that part, and to this day she still has those scars. It's something she will always remember, because the scars are visible and she can see them every time she looks in the mirror. Now the good thing is that my daughter is a bighearted kid who always finds a way to make things better. Since then, she has sought out her own remedies for removing the scars, learned to live with them, and understands that these scars don't define her.

Like my daughter, many of us have sores that leave scars, whether they are physical, mental, emotional, or spiritual. When we are young girls, often we can rise above the scar, but as a grown woman sometimes it is very hard to do so.

Let's recap what the doctor told me. He said that my daughter's scars would diminish a bit with time and that I would have to take the action step of getting medication and applying it. It is important to take note of this, because it is foundational when it comes to healing. Healing really does take time. It can't be rushed, and it has to have a starting point. I wish I had purchased that medication, because I can only imagine what the progress could have been. My heart breaks over this, y'all, 'cause I could have done something. For a couple of years, I blamed myself for her scars. It's not my fault that she has these scars, but it is definitely my responsibility as a mother to make sure my kids get the help they need.

We have to acknowledge any area of our life that needs healing and pursue it. The good news for you is that God sent me ahead of you so you can learn from my mistakes. Here are some valuable lessons I have learned:

- When someone offers a solution, don't ignore it. If an expert gives you advice, they probably know what they are talking about, so you need to consider how this advice can work for you.

- Whenever there is an opportunity to help yourself or someone else, be the first in line to volunteer.

Let's talk about healing for a bit. The root word that it is derived from is the Old English term *haelen*, meaning "wholeness." It means to develop a sense of personal wholeness that involves the physical, mental, emotional, social, and spiritual aspects of the human experience. It is an intervention, an outcome, and a process. Wholeness is what everybody wants. It is the beauty of every human being.

Can you imagine having some of your body parts at someone else's house? That sounds absurd, right? It's impossible! Or is it? I beg to differ. We leave our emotions with other people and at other places all the time. If you have ever had an argument with someone and did not resolve it, it's very likely that your body suffered. Part of your emotions were left at the scene, and the other part went home with you. Very often, the person you had your encounter with is also carrying the emotional trauma with them. There are so many examples of this, like a misunderstanding with a teacher at school regarding your kid. Or the countless times you were on the phone with a customer service rep and the call did not go as planned. Maybe someone treated you unfairly. What about the person who cut you off on the road? How about something said to you that was insensitive? Any of these could create an unhealthy reaction, leaving you spiritually punctured with emotions leaking out everywhere. I can recall some of these experiences myself on many occasions. It's like leaving your heart at a grocery store, your mind in the car, and your body at home. That's not wholeness.

One of the biggest things I had to realize before I could truly experience healing was knowing that I needed it. Before, I thought I could overcome all of my life battles by myself. That was a mistake that I had to learn from. I want to talk about this for a bit, because I know that many of us have some life experiences that we are currently dealing with, like unresolved hurt, loss of relationships, injustice, being mistreated, or the pain of our past. These things are still lingering, and I want to encourage you to start looking at your situation as a possible need for healing. Big reactions and situations that are still present are healing screams for help. The time is now, today, because each day that you have air flowing through your lungs is the perfect day to create a space for healing.

When I finally received some help, things started to get better for me. Now, I can't imagine my life without getting help from others. I need it. I strongly recommend that you make getting help a part of your life. It's one of the best decisions you could ever make, and it must become one of your golden rules. Healing is a journey that requires you to travel with your entire being. It will not settle for pieces of you but is craving to have your all. Pain can leave a scar, and healing is the remedy. Healing is the participation of choosing yourself. Are you willing to do all that it takes for your own personal healing?

Back in 2014, when I walked into a therapy office, I was so uncomfortable because I knew I was troubled deep down inside my soul. I had the emotional scars to prove it. Though I was functioning in many ways, and it appeared that I was thriving and living well, I was far from it internally. There were unresolved and unsettled situations in my life. I had a hole in my own wholeness and was in need of a healing hope. Sitting across the room from my therapist while she asked me several questions revealed a lot to me. I discovered that I had not taken care of the little girl inside me. As a woman, I focused only on nurturing my adult self. I never considered helping my younger self. It was this place in my life where I needed to integrate my young girl with my big girl self. I realized that I had been operating on autopilot for a long time. I have always prided myself on being strong, but sometimes that can be my cover-up. With many years of practicing incompleteness, I had become skilled at existing in a way that appeared to be whole.

There is nothing wrong with being a strong woman. She is powerful! So let's give a shout-out to the strong women we know who have been through some things and didn't let anything take them down. Some of you reading this know it's who you are, and I applaud you. Strength is what we all need so that we can keep on growing. However, it would be good for us to acknowledge that strength has many layers. I will never invalidate the gift of strength, but I will always challenge where we think our strength should come from. My strength was laced with my hard work ethics, accomplishments, and being able to overcome some really difficult things in my life. These are all so very good. On the other hand, the lack of healing in my life would reveal a different kind of strength that I would need to acquire. And I am convinced that every woman must learn the two sides of strength in order to fully live the kind of life that honors her heart, soul, mind and body. When I realized this, I decided to pursue healing for myself.

I remember reading 2 Corinthians 12:10 (ESV) and trying to comprehend these words about strength: "For when I am weak, then I am strong." This did not make any sense to me. How can a person be strong in their weakness all at the same time? It was a foreign concept. Nobody ever taught me anything about being weak. If this is a prerequisite for a relationship with God, then we are gonna have to do some renegotiation. Weakness is not something I'm familiar with. Women of strength don't do weak!

Anyhoo, as I continued to read, I noticed that a weakness was all the hardships Paul had been through or was going through. This was a real person dealing with some real stuff like you and me, and he understood his need for help. In my past experiences—from physical and mental abuse to spiritual misuse such as bodily harm, betrayal, lies, mental manipulation, insults, biblical bullying, and injustice—I could relate to being weak. All of the pain growing up, my young adult years, to the experiences in my church were no different from one another in the fact that it all left me devastated. Many people tried to give me their thoughts on how to deal with my pain. I had been told things like, "You need to pray about it," "You got to let it go and move on with your life," and, "It happened to me too." Though some folks meant well, their comments sucked. I was not at a place where I could receive any of it, even if some of it was true.

Life happens to all of us, and sometimes it's just not fair. But that does not mean that we have to accept useless comments as the answer to our situation. No, ma'am! We will not sweep this under the rug. If you or anybody you know has experienced cruel and sinful acts done against them, you do not deserve to be told to just let it go. What in the heck does that mean, anyway, when the fact is that you can't let go of something you never had a hold of? However, the real issue is that pain can have a hold on us, and we have to seek the healing that releases that hold.

Let me take you back to the therapist's office, because I want to invite you into this space fully. When I went in to see my therapist, I was what some folks would call a tough cookie. I came in strong. She asked questions; I answered. Every moment was a matter-of-fact situation. I was not going to give her anything more than what she asked, and even then I would not go beyond the surface. Here's the deal, y'all: I'm the one who called searching for someone who could help me 'cause I knew I needed it. You know when you know, right? However, my approach to my therapy experience was guarded. I did not see that I was weak and in need of help. It would take me three visits before the walls would come down. On that third visit, she looked me in the eye, and the first thing she said was, "I believe that you have been hurt, and all that you shared with me is true." She went on to say, "I want to validate all of it." It was the first time that anyone had ever said that to me.

Another challenge I suffered was my own inner thoughts. The way we think about ourselves and our situation is one of the most challenging areas of healing. I thought that I should be over it because it happened so long ago. I thought I was supposed to have more strength than what I possessed at the time. Thoughts like these minimize your pain and clutter your soul. They keep you in a perpetual spin. Your inner monologue becomes the story you tell yourself and everyone else. If you struggle with your thoughts, please talk to someone who can help you.

I have discovered three levels of strength that have benefited me in so many ways in my healing journey.

1. The first phase of strength is *awareness*. Getting in touch with the why, what, and how you think about yourself is crucial. Our thinking creates the most damage on the path to healing. It's because our mind carries all of the turmoil. Though your body may recover, the scar is still visible because the mind struggles in the here and now. It can recall every moment into existence, illuminating the incident as if it was present and it is—in your mind. One of the ways you can train your mind is by doing exercises that will strengthen your thought process. Taking the time daily to train your thoughts is a good and healthy practice. Standing up to those thoughts that are not helpful will prove to be successful over time. My mind care practice was essential to my healing process. This is the kind of attention to self that is necessary for your growth.

2. The second phase of strength is *admitting* you are weak. To be weak is to experience sickness. It could be

anywhere inside the mind, body and soul. In my case, all of the above were affected. However, the most significant area of focus for me was spiritually. I was ill spiritually. I was so sick that physically my body began to ache. This was my truth. Sometimes we are afraid of admitting the truth because of this false idea that saying you are weak actually weakens you even more. That's a bald-faced lie. We have to destigmatize this thought process. This is genuinely an experience we will all cross paths with. We need to live in reality and stay present. Facing the things that we need to accept leads us to addressing the problem, helping us to be overcomers in our situation.

3. The third level of strength is to take *action*. What area of your life is screaming out for healing, and what are you going to do about it? Don't let any more of your time expire without doing something with it. Time is inevitably passing, and all you have is the one second you have now. Do you need to have a conversation with yourself? You know, the one where you need to challenge yourself? When was the last time you wrote down what you need to take care of? What's on your to-do list? Is there a call you need to make? If there is an appointment you need to schedule, put this book down right now and do it and come back after you have done so. Don't delay these action steps. When people procrastinate, they are intentionally committing to being stagnant, complacent, and unproductive. You have to have the kind of hope that leads your healing. And you have to be proactive in the process. Your healing is mandatory! It must become the assignment that you are diligent to take on. It has to be the class you major in with plans to graduate.

Lastly, there is something that you need to know that is very important. When you decide to get help for you, you may experience a pushback from yourself and others. You may go through some situations where you might act out a bit. Reminiscing on pain or regurgitating the past can bring out some ugly. Don't be afraid or alarmed. It's the process. I remember some people in my life would look at my behavior and decide for themselves who I was. They judged me from head to toe. Because they forgot their own flaws, it was easy to look at mine. If you have ever been summed up, you know how hurtful it is. It's so hard when we go through this. But I want to remind you where to put your energy: on your own healing. It really doesn't matter what everyone else thinks about you. You have to choose not to care.

One of the things I love about my favorite singer, Tina Turner, is how she did not let the pain in her life dictate who she became. We also have this amazing opportunity to turn our trials into a testimony. This is your moment, this is your chance, this is your time. Everything you have been through is ready to be cared for by you. You have to decide if you will be the one who passes your legacy on. Do not ignore the silent cry, the thick thoughts, and the overwhelming emotional explosion inside you . And just so you know, there is nothing wrong with an explosion as long as it is the fireworks of your life that are bursting in celebration of you happily healing.

CHAPTER SIX

FORGIVENESS

"Declutter the dust from your soul."

Have you heard the saying, "The best is yet to come?" I heard it many times, but I have to be honest: for a long time, I never embraced this idea for myself. I felt like folks were just saying a bunch of "blah, blah, blah," talking out of the side of their necks. Y'all know those people who want to motivate you like influencers, motivational speakers, coaches, preachers, teachers, the gurus of the century, or heroes of a lifetime. They mean well. Of course, they have our best interests in mind, and we appreciate them. Why else would we take time out of our schedules to go and listen to them for hours upon hours? It's because somewhere deep down inside of us, we believe they have answers for our situation.

We value learning from the experts. We are hopeful that it is possible we will experience something that will help us. I have attended several church services, events, seminars, and conferences with a room full of people all excited and chanting every word the speaker told them to say. The speaker gets everyone all hyped up, saying stuff like, "If you want to be great then you have to tap into your GREATNESS." These catchy phrases pumped me up, but in the back of my mind, I'd be thinking, *How in the world do I do that?* First of all, no one had ever told me I was great, so I knew nothing about greatness. Can any of y'all relate? Then, after all the hoopla, comes the final punchline, the mighty formula to solve all my problems. So, I write it down. I love writing down stuff. My journal is full of amazing quotes, advice, and inspirational words from some incredible people. So far, so good—until the seminar was over. I'd apply what I learned for a few weeks, and then it was back to the real me. The real me gets excited about an adventure until it comes to an end. Then I am bored and looking for another purpose in life.

Do you ever struggle with boredom? Do you lose interest in something and then start doing something else? Are you prone to not finishing what you start? Taking on a new thing and being excited about it is a wonderful thing. What is not good is the lack of follow through. For years I struggled with most of the above. But therapy taught me many things, including to examine all of my options and to do the work of decluttering the dust from my soul.

A very familiar word kept showing up on my journey—"forgiveness." Forgiveness is the action or process of forgiving or being forgiven. It is the ability to cease feeling resentment against someone. If you struggle with any of the above, have you considered the possibility that there could be a lack of forgiveness of yourself or someone else? Dig into this with me for a moment. Allow yourself time to examine your situation. I read an article in *Psychology Today* that stated, "To actually forgive, one would need to release resentment or anger." To release is to set free or let go of. Releasing something or setting someone free is therapeutic and it creates a pathway for healing. It cleanses the soul when we let go of all things that threaten our internal freedom.

Did you know that a lack of forgiveness hinders you more than the person you haven't forgiven? It keeps you trapped in an inner turmoil of emotions. Forgiveness is vitally important for mental wellness. It propels people forward rather than keeping them emotionally engaged in an injustice or trauma. It has been shown to elevate mood, enhance optimism, and guard against anger, stress, anxiety, and depression. I bet some of you are thinking, "How is forgiveness attached to seminars and boredom?" Well, if you are wondering about this, I am glad, because this is the part where I will share an analogy that may be helpful for you.

Are you familiar with the principle of cause and effect? A cause is an action and the effect is the resulting reaction. Example: eating something you know is not good for you is the action and an upset stomach is the effect. A scripture that speaks a little more to this concept is Galatians 6:7, which says, "You reap what you sow." It's the process of what you plant and what is produced from what you planted. The reason I would get so bored after these events is because I wasn't sowing the kind of seeds that would grow. I wasn't planting properly. The seminars were quick fixes. They had no depth beyond the day they existed. It's not because the speakers were not good or the facilities, food, or itineraries were horrible. The problem was that I did not have a plan for myself beyond the event. I never thought about what I wanted to do with the information I received. Nor did I consider what I would have to do differently in order to receive the full opportunities that awaited me. The other challenge for me is that I had so much internal work still to be done. The information from all those seminars fell on the soil of a heart that couldn't receive all that it was capable of because it was blocked by unforgiveness.

Unforgiveness can be tricky. Have you ever heard someone say, "I forgive you but I won't forget it"? They are basically saying the words but are housing unforgiveness in their mind, perhaps to keep for later. Honestly, this is a fruitless lifeline that many people hold onto. It's a cheap way to express forgiveness. It's powerless and doesn't help anybody. In fact, it keeps coming back every time another situation arises where they have to forgive. They will say this same phrase again, thinking that they have actively forgiven someone when they have not.

Then there are other folks who just ignore or hide their need to forgive. Those who do so operate dysfunctionally and don't realize it's deception. It has deep roots, and unless it is uprooted, it will grow bigger and bigger and eventually expose all the cracks in their life.

Let me tell you about the power unforgiveness has over you. It will torture, confuse, and abuse you. It is designed to make you a hostage, keep you entangled, and put bars over your heart, confining you in your own prison. I know this because it has been a struggle for me most of my life, and I have felt its effect on me. It convinced me to make those who had harmed me pay, so I spent a lot of my good energy doing this, not realizing how much time I had wasted. Y'all, this is not an easy subject for me. As I write this, it gives me chills, because I remember what it was like when I did not forgive. It was so painful. I became cynical, bitter, and paranoid. I was falling all over the place in my life.

When I became a mother, it got real personal. I started watching every man and woman when they were around my kids. I made sure they maintained a distance, a lot of distance. I created a defensive wall for everyone around me. My kids suffered the consequences as well. They were not allowed opportunities to build relationships because I would not let them get too close to anyone unless I was present. I was scared and had trained my mind to believe everyone was a potential threat. I had placed my trauma over my own kids. It would take years for me to see the effects of my decisions. This is the part of my story that actually breaks my heart, but I am grateful that I know a better way now. Let me be clear about something, though: there are situations where we need to be cautious and careful. Because of everything I experienced, it was important for me to keep my girls safe, but it was not okay for me to shelter them because of my own pain.

You may not struggle with forgiveness like I did, but I can say this much: the signs of it are obvious. So, if you ever think you can mask it well and no one can see it, I'm here to tell you this stuff leaks out. I can actually spot it a mile away, because I had all of the symptoms that showcased my lack of it. You also might not want to forgive because you think the perpetrator must pay for all that they did. You personally want to make him or her suffer because that's what they deserve. I feel you on this. A few years ago, I would be at the party with you, celebrating crucifying the person for what they had done. However, when we do this, we nurse the pain so tightly that it sticks to us like glue, causing our lives to be sticky for everyone we come in contact with. I don't know about you but I don't think anyone who values relationships would volunteer to be in a sticky situation. Why do we spend our precious time in this vicious, debilitating cycle when it has not made us better? Unfortunately, it's one of the things that keeps us cluttered. If we want more for ourselves, we have to forgive.

I studied many scriptures about this subject matter. These scriptures have become my best weapon against anything that seeks to suffocate my soul. I am very clear on the strategies of a thief. "He comes to steal, kill and destroy" (John 10:10). Sis, don't let unforgiveness keep stealing from you. Start forgiving and get your life back. Someone once asked me, "How do you know if you have not forgiven someone?" At the time, I could not answer, but after spending many years on lockdown and unable to reach my highest self, I found the answer for me. I know I have not forgiven when I talk about what happened to me and it leaves me depleted of my energy. Also, when it feels fresh, like it happened yesterday. It shows up in rage, frustration with others, bitterness, a lack of trust, and how you treat others.

When I think about what others have done to me, I have to also consider what I have done to others. Some of us are really good people and have good intensions, and we might think we don't go around hurting others. But you and I know that is not true. Everyone has hurt someone in some way. If I did a roll call for all the people I have hurt, folks would be lining up. I am sure a few people would line up for you as well. None of us are perfect. Anytime you are in a relationship—and that applies to all of us—we end up doing things that may be hurtful to someone else.

Have you ever had an interaction with someone and it got heated really fast? Like when someone cut in line in front of you or the person at the coffee shop accidentally gave you the wrong drink and you got upset? Sometimes we react to situations at a level ten when they are actually a level zero. Some folks justify their case of going to the extreme emotionally with the argument that they are righteous for justice. Or they don't take no mess from nobody. Maybe it's that they have a conviction to stand up for themselves. The latter can be a positive reinforcement for healthy boundaries. However, any extreme reaction is a warning sign. This is a huge indicator there is pain present and in need of healing and forgiveness. There are also people who are always on the defensive, ready to fight and protect themselves and everybody else that they care about. They throw swing after swing but never see their own knockout coming.

Unforgiveness is a knockout. It throws many punches and actually brings more harm to those who keep it for themselves. It creates a strong reaction and is usually linked to a pain point. A pain point is a recurring source of trouble. When it comes to unforgiveness, you can be sure that if you talk about an issue that has not been forgiven, it still hurts because it's a touchy subject. When there is a news highlight about a similar story, you are the advocate for justice. The storyline of a book that sounds like yours deeply touches your heart. It's your experience, and you know it so well. There is a passion that comes alive because of it.

I love passionate people. Many of them are going to make so much change in our world. However, we must get in touch with our need to forgive and never let misguided passions thwart our personal growth. Is there anyone you need to forgive? Is there something that you regret? Do you need to forgive yourself? How will you know that you have forgiven? It is a good thing to find answers to these critical questions. Whatever your answers are, I want you to know that you have the capability to forgive.

Forgiveness is an ingredient for life. When you forgive, you make a deposit and investment in yourself, and this is a huge win. I am a fan of self-help, self-development, and self-growth application. These systems help us learn how to forgive ourselves and others. We need it! It is the kind of spiritual cleansing that needs to take place, because if this stuff just sits in your soul, it's bound to take you down with it. And we are not signing up for that.

Just like you sweep dust off the floor when you clean your house, you have to do the same thing internally. One of the ways you can start decluttering the dust is to admit it's there. Second, start cleaning up your mindset about it. It's not supposed to govern your thoughts. Be proactive and discover new ways of thinking about your situation. There is so much research about this subject because it's one of the largest areas of life work people have to explore on a daily basis.

There are people in your life right now that are ready to help you. If you have even a hint of unforgiveness and are bound by the things that have caused you pain and you are unwilling to deal with them, no one will be able to effectively assist you. You can go to seminar after seminar, and at the end of it, you will come right back to the same place in your life.

Here is a challenge for you: Google forgiveness. Choose one article that specifically talks about the benefits of forgiveness. Take one benefit and start implementing a habit that will assist you. For example, if it says it lowers the risk of heart attacks (which, by the way, it does), do something that helps you take care of your heart. Perhaps meditation or going on a walk can be beneficial for you. This will help create the kind of space in your life for good, healthy movement that actually helps you get rid of the dust and prepares you to work on forgiving. I don't like being morbid, but I don't want to sugarcoat this. Dust belongs over coffins that are six feet under and on dirt roads. Dust is only powerful when it is being formed into something good, like when God made Adam. Other than that, it blows with the wind as it should. I don't want you or anyone to have a dusty soul. But it doesn't matter what I want. It is really all about what you want.

Forgiveness is something you will have to come to terms with. I will also say this: "What will you lose by taking a chance on you?" Nothing! This is all a gain for you. Forgiveness is the gift that you can always give yourself. So, sis, start passing out those presents.

CHAPTER SEVEN

UNDERSTANDING YOUR WORTH

"Fitting in is not an option, but being yourself is."

I live loved because "I am loved" is a new mantra that I chose for myself at the beginning of the pandemic. The world was faced with uncertainties and unknowns. No one could predict or determine what would happen next. I felt like every living soul was at a standstill, in a desperate state. Our lives were at stake. Many of us lost loved ones unexpectedly. Social injustice was loud and overwhelming, and pain was almost unbearable. Political propaganda was on the forefront, pulling the attention of anyone who was interested. The world was in an uproar and I chose to be intentional by taking care of and loving myself during these times.

I found myself questioning a lot during this time. What do you do when the entire world seems to be collapsing? Do I run and hide? Should I find a group to connect with? Maybe I should get my family and move? There were a lot of possible options, but the one thing that kept staring me in the face was to know my WORTH. Worth is one's own value as a human being. It is the fabric of your soul. When life moves, and it moves fast, you have to decide what you are going to do and who you want to be doing it with. The world was not going to change or stop for me. These times were some of the hardest. I had all kinds of mixed emotions. There were many moments when I just cried as I watched the big divide in this world. I found myself in conversations that were strange and toxic all at the same time.

Some folks thought that I was rather nonchalant because I wasn't fighting for their cause, while others were afraid to even make eye contact with me because they didn't know where I stood or who's side I was on. My church tried to address some of the issues, but I felt the church was inexperienced and knew nothing about how to deal with these matters—and neither did I. For a while, I became silent. I stopped talking. I would just listen to everything around me.

Thank God for a few good friends in my life at that time who assisted me in my life journey not to lose hope. I stayed in prayer and read my Bible daily. I got focused and channeled my energy into getting direction from God. This is where I was able to find some peace in an unpeaceful world. There was never a moment that I did not care about what was going on in the world. It pained me greatly. But I was clear on my assignment through it all. It did not matter what others thought, because their opinion of me was fruitless and it would never benefit me to care. I discovered that silence was a blessing so that I could listen to God. I decided to grow my faith rather than fight somebody else's fight. I dedicated my allegiance to

God rather than my attention to man. I also participated in an online self-development program which helped me get specific about what I wanted to work on in my life. Many times, I heard the phrase, "Don't waste anything." This became a signature phrase for me and a new hope. I tucked this little quote right in my heart, and it has been serving me ever since. I made some great choices for myself and I watched my own transformation during a very difficult season for the entire world.

Are you still with me? I need you to be all in for what I am about to say next. I want to refer back to a scripture from my introduction, Genesis 1:26-27 (ESV), which says, "Then God said, 'Let us make man in our image, after our likeness….' in the image of God he created him; male and female he created them." I have read this scripture many times, but it never impacted me like it did during the pandemic because this time when I read it I received a fresh new perspective about life.

We are all here intentionally. I was made with and for a purpose. Therefore, I will live from this place of existence. Y'all, we come from Him who is great, gracious, and good all at the same time. God placed value on our lives from the beginning of creation. I decided to claim my value during a time when we were all trying to figure out the next phase of an uncertain life. Focusing on my worth during this time gave me a sense of belonging and empowered me to be courageous and bold in my life. I really understood that I only had one life to live, so I was going to do it well.

There is something about choosing you. It gives you the freedom to be fully you and not be swayed to hop on the bandwagon of something or someone else's idea of what you should be doing. You don't get caught up in everybody else's stuff when you know who you are. My purpose is not the same as everybody else's, and the same applies to you. God has called each of us to something specific. Becoming aware of the deception and unhealthy influences that exist will help you navigate the direction of your life. Learning to value who you are gives you the strength to stay grounded and live in your worth. You always have to go back to your own value system. *Fitting in is not an option, but being yourself is.*

Before I move ahead, I want to put this out there: I am not making light of the heartbreaking events of the pandemic. That is not what this is about. This is about paying close attention to your life and your reactions to what is happening in it. It is about living in a continual rhythm of knowing, growing, and glowing. Living in your worth is mandatory, but in order to do so, you need to know when you are *not* living in your worth.

Here are some things that I did or saw other people get caught up in. They are what I call "worth killers," and they strip a person down to their bare bones.

- Getting entangled in the affairs of the world – You are bothered by everything that goes on around you. Taking on other people's problems. You think negatively. You can't sleep. Anger is your reaction, and bitterness is your buddy.

- Doing what other people do because it's the trend – All of your friends cut their hair, and you do it too because you don't want to be left out, so you casually clone yourself.

- The influences of the media – Whatever they say, you do it.

- Absorbing other people's lives - Focusing on things you can't change. Trying to control other people's behavior and what they have chosen to do with their lives. Feeling the need to respond to everything someone else says.

- Seeking approval or permission from others – Asking people what they think about your talents. Not making a decision because you are waiting for someone else to tell you what, when, and how to do it.

- Living your life through and for others – Building your life around your spouse or children. They are your life force.

- Wanting to be liked – The need to be accepted. Inserting yourself into every conversation or situation.

- Misplaced values – Dismissal of your standards. Settling for less. Making unhealthy compromises.

- Copying other people's ideas and making them your own – Duplicating someone else's life. Resisting your own gifts and embracing someone else's. Diminishing the value inside you.

- Shell Existing – Waking up every day without purpose. The lack of good energy flowing through the body because you are angry, mad, sad, and afraid.

When any of these become a lifestyle, it is a huge indicator that there is a chasm in your soul. These worth killers can distract anyone at any time, which is why we must take a closer look at what is happening in our lives.

Previously, I mentioned the abuse that took place when I was a young child. I want to go back to that so I can move you forward into this moment. The things that happened to you or me do not devalue or compromise our worth. Our value is still solid and strong. But sometimes things from the past come back to disrupt our lives. When we understand our worth, we will not tolerate any deceptive activity that tries to crush who we are.

Next, you must also be in tune with what is helpful for you and what is not. This is a great go-to whenever you face challenges. Think about what has worked well for you in the past. What helped you get through a difficult situation? Write it down as a living in your worth experience.

I have listed a few ways that have been helpful and life-changing for me. Hopefully they can also help you.

- Standing up for yourself – You don't let people mistreat you. RESPECT is your standard. You are willing to speak your truth.

- Soul/Self-care – Doing something for yourself consistently. Taking care of the way you think and feel. Getting help if you need it.

- Making commitments to yourself and others – Following through on what you said you would do. Be a person of your word.

- Saying NO often – You don't do everything people want you to do. You have boundaries.

- Loyalty to self – You can count on you. Belief in yourself. Making good decisions.

- No self-discrimination – You do not insult yourself. There is no condemnation of you or others.

- Life management – Choose valuable and healthy options that work for you. Get rid of things that you don't need. You get rest for your heart, mind, and soul. The ability to stop when needed. Make the most of your time.

- Character growth – Stay honest and true to yourself. Dismiss all negativity. Build healthy relationships. Practice what you preach. Live with integrity. Do something new. Be intentional. Express gratitude.

One of the biggest reasons why women do not live their highest good is because they don't have higher standards for themselves. In many ways, they don't really believe anything is beyond where they are at. Ladies, this is not true. When you start feeling like this, shift your mindset and explore the situation at hand. Get involved with yourself by digging into the facts, find your truths, and start reminding yourself of how valuable you truly are.

To shift my mindset, I like to evaluate my life by breaking it down into three body parts so that I can be aware of what part or if all parts need adjusting in any given situation. Consider this analogy so that you can get specific: head center, middle control, and the torso below effect.

HEAD CENTER

One of the biggest problems that people encounter is adding unnecessary challenges to their lives by the way they think. It starts right at the top. The head center is where your brain lives. It is the place where your mindset is shaped. The things you believe, feel, say, and think are all hanging out there. What have you told yourself about you? Or, better yet, who are you listening to that thinks they know you better than you? Our belief system is how we show up everywhere we go. For example, if you believe you are unworthy, you will live an unworthy life. Sometimes our mind can be a bully, a backstabber, or, in a good situation, a bestie. When the bully and backstabber show up, you have to challenge your belief system. Ask yourself, *How is this possible? When did it happen? What confirms it?* You need to be able to answer when those negative thoughts come and try to devalue your existence. God was very clear when he created you. I guarantee you if you start to stand up to these attacks, you will find yourself winning all of the time.

Have you ever watched two people arguing? It's so unsettling, because you don't know what will happen from one moment to the next. Everybody nearby could possibly be on the radar for some trouble. And if the argument gets too loud, you might rush out of the area and find your safe place. This is a situation you have no control over, so you would most likely focus on protecting yourself. It's your natural instinct. You value your life, so you are not going to stay in any situation that would put you in danger.

What if we applied this same instinct when we hear the insults of our mind? How about protecting yourself from yourself? Just like you would respond to an unsafe physical situation, you can do the same with your mind. Our bodies have many parts, and it is good for us to nurture every part. If the brain is not nourished well, it will cause problems in the rest of the body. But when it is pampered and cared for, it tells the rest of the body how awesome it is. Your mind will become your bestie when you make it a self-soul care priority.

There was a time when I neglected my mind. I am a singer, and when I perform I love the encouragement from hearing how much people enjoyed the performance. But I remember a time when I was booed. It took everything within me not to break down and cry. That booing situation put a lot of fear in me, and I developed a codependent spirit where I began to seek compliments from the people closest to me. If my mama didn't tell me the show was good, then it wasn't good. If my friends had no comments and just smiled because they wanted to make nice with me, then I felt like I had not done a great job. If they didn't say I killed it, I would feel like a mediocre performer. Those experiences shaped my mind, and I behaved accordingly.

Do you see how compelling the mind is? It is so easy to get caught up like a spinning wheel. Eventually you will feel yourself spiraling, and it can be so overwhelming. We must be careful about the unhealthy ways we think. Our mind is the part of our body that we need to spend a lot of time building, nurturing, and growing. When we do this, we develop a healthy pattern of reshifting and gifting ourselves. If I looked more at the success I was having as a singer rather than at what people thought about my singing, I would have been pampering my mind. Some things that I do now to take care of myself as an artist is reflecting on the hard work that I put in for every performance. Next, I enjoy my performances. I see the beauty in the art that I am creating, and I celebrate it. I don't ask people how they enjoyed the show anymore. I do want them to have a great time. But whether they think my show is good or not is not my concern. I give my all to it, and that is good enough for me. This is my current situation, y'all.

We give people too much access to our lives, and some things are just not for them. You are not responsible for what someone else does or does not like. You have enough on your hands, and it's called your own life. So, stop worrying about what other people think. They don't get to approve you. Anytime you find yourself seeking validation or confirmation, go back to the original construction. You were made in God's likeness. The people of the world, the lookie-loos, they are just spectators. They have no say over you. Even your family and friends cannot place value on you. They are the "additionals" in your life whose purpose is being your support system and fans. This is a blessing, so thank God for the blessing.

Hear me on this! Your worth is what you were born with. So let your authentic self shine!

MIDDLE CONTROL

Middle control is your gut instincts. Your heart and the rest of your organs are here. It's your core. It is what supports the head center and the torso below. Without it, the body could not exist. It's here where you can sense that trouble awaits. You can feel it in your body when something is off and not right.

Y'all, I can't express this enough: if you don't let this part assist you, then your body will have chest pains, backaches, cramps, indigestion, stomachaches, deterioration, illnesses with no name, and, for some folks, the inability to control their own body fluids when this area is unhealthy and ignored.

Don't dismiss what is happening inside of you. You have intuition for a reason. It is there to help you live a healthy life.

TORSO AND BELOW

Torso and below is the place where you surrender your weight, because it can hold you up. Physically, it carries you from place to place. It is flexible and knows how to maneuver things when needed. It enjoys the walk of life. The torso it is known as the human trunk. It does not need other parts of the body, such as arms or legs, to function. It is a foundational part of the body. All of the structures below it are like stabilizers, keeping it balanced.

This is the part of the body responsible for movement. Just like the natural steps of humanity that take place from the phase of a baby's first steps to adult life, we all desire to walk. As we get older, there will be a time when some of us will not be able to physically walk and take advantage of the steps available to us, which is why we have to take them now. Living in our worth is not for tomorrow but for today. When God created the earth, he made every provision for you to live in your worth.

UNBLOCK ME

My husband bought me a book called *Girl, Stop Apologizing* by Rachel Hollis. The book sat on my table for weeks until I finally decided to open it. I immediately became interested in the subject matter. First off, I noticed that she lived in Texas, which is where I am from. I always love when I cross paths with a Texas trailblazer. I was sure that I would be able to relate to this woman, and I did.

I read something amazing that I will never forget. In one of the chapters in her book, she asked the reader to write a letter to themselves. I thought it was a bit corny and silly. My mind couldn't comprehend how this would help me. It took me a few months before I followed through and did it. It turned out to be one of the most amazing things I could do for myself. I had never done anything like it. It actually enhanced my view of myself and deepened my conviction that God had made me amazing. Another thing is that doing this allowed me to create a practical support system for myself. I can reflect on this letter at any time to help me when I think or feel insecure or doubtful of myself. Choosing to take an action step helped me to develop a new habit. I am now able to affirm what I know to be true about me.

Affirmations have become a very influential tool for me. If you don't have an affirmation template, it is a must-have. Twenty years ago, we did not have the kind of tools we have today. Nowadays, you can go on the internet and listen to a great pep talk and quickly be inspired. It's pretty awesome. I have become the kind of girl who seeks inspiration for myself. Though I appreciate whenever some amazing person encourages me, I am not waiting for it.

There are times when I thought to myself, *What if I was the only girl on the earth? How would I survive?* And the answer is I'd have to figure it out. Because God gave me this amazing mind, I am always thinking of creative ways to empower myself. Ladies, we must to do this for ourselves! Make it a daily decision to see your worth and remind yourself that you are worthy.

Whenever in doubt, there are three ways you can start building yourself up: by imagining, writing, and creating a reminder. Create your own affirmation template. Start with using your search engine. Look for a free thirty-day calendar and download it. Choose a time of the day that you will commit to writing an inspirational word of your choice on this calendar every day for thirty days. I recommend using ink. The writing will give you the ability to feel it in your hands. Once it's complete, keep it in a visible place so you can see it daily.

Another practice you can do is sit still for fifteen minutes and allow your mind to imagine your possibilities. Think of things that are positive. What are some ways you can encourage yourself? Write it down and create a plan to do it. Make it a habit to affirm yourself daily. Never negotiate your worth because your value is priceless. Every morning when you wake up, and every evening before you go to bed, look in the mirror and say, "I am enough, and I have always been enough."

CHAPTER EIGHT

REMARKABLE YOU

"Embrace the flashlight of your soul"

Do you remember in school when you had to take tests? The room would be so quiet that you could hear a pin drop. Then there was that teacher—we all get one, you know, the one that walks around the room to see who could possibly be cheating? It was like you had been convicted before proven guilty. I never understood why they did that, because it usually caused so much anxiety for kids who were already afraid of failing the test. The test itself was enough pressure. All of those ridiculous questions you had to answer that never came up again in real-life situations. On the other hand, some of us had teachers who could care less. They were the ones who would be reading their magazines while you were sweating like a rotisserie chicken.

    I dreaded taking tests. It was one of the most challenging things for me. On test day, I felt like my heart rate paced at one hundred miles per hour, especially when it was a timed test. I did not like being timed for anything. In reality, taking tests is an ongoing life practice. We took tests in school, and life will bring us many more. Though I did not like taking tests, it prepared me for life. It taught me preparation, discipline, and to value time. If I understand these basic principles, I can learn how to manage my life well.

One cool thing about school is that we get the opportunity to study. You and I both were given this task. Were you the one who spent your time in the library on your lunch break? Or were you, like me, someone who waited till the night before to open the notes from the week before? I love focused, dedicated, inquisitive folks who take the time to do everything possible to be and do their best. They inspire me so much. If you were and still are a hardworking student, I applaud you, because you made the choice to be. We are all human beings capable of doing incredible things, but will we consistently choose it for ourselves?

Life can also be likened to doing homework. You have to do it, turn it in, and wait for the grade. It's very similar to the same process as being in school. One of my best friends and I joke a lot about turning ourselves in. We do this when we know we have done something that we just need to come clean about, like not being neat and fancy homemakers. We understand cleaning, but our skills in this department are not at the top of the list. And don't talk to us about hanging our clothes up every day, because that is not on our to-do list. Between us, we probably have at least seven hundred clothing items. In a situation like this, the choice is obvious, but sometimes you just don't take care of what is right in front of you. The two of us get each other, but we knew that we had to get rid of some stuff. So, we turned ourselves in, because we couldn't continue flunking this subject of our lives. Two garage sales later, I ended up at the local thrift shop, where I dropped off my items and hers.

Y'all, class is always in session, whether you are in a physical school or not. When was the last time you turned yourself in? If you want to be excellent in every area of your life, I have some suggestions that will help you ace your next life test.

First, start doing the math. We all know that one plus one equals two, right? There is no way of getting around this truth. It's the same when it comes to living our lives. You plus you equals YOU. You can add up the experiences in your life, the people in your circle, the job you have, the kids you birthed, the husband you've been married to for years, the career you have chosen, and all of your other achievements, and you will always be the sum of it all. *You* are the common denominator. Everywhere you go, you will be there. So, keep that in mind in everything you do.

Second, when it's dark, get a flashlight! Y'all, I don't like being in the dark. It's kinda spooky for me. But on a dark night, I keep a nightlight on so I can see where I am going. There is something about being able to see things that otherwise would be unfamiliar and unknown if left in the dark. It's like being blindfolded and trying to walk across the street in oncoming traffic. Sounds kinda foolish to do, right?

The truth is that some of us approach life like this. We step out into the dark without our flashlight. Like when we say yes to things that we don't know if we can complete. Or doing things at the last minute, when you could have done it two weeks ago. We are setting ourselves up for dark moments when we approach life like this. The courses of our lives can be difficult, but the beauty of it all is that we get to study. Studying yourself gives you the ability to know yourself well. When was the last time you took the time to discover something new about you?

During the time I attended the self-development course, I got to journal pivotal events of my life that happened to me from a young girl to becoming an adult. I got to see all the good and the ugly all at once. When I first started this journey, I was excited—until I got to the hard part. I said to myself, *I am not doing this. Why is this even a part of this course? I dealt with this stuff already. Who wants to rehash painful moments of their life?* Well, even though sometimes I can be stubborn, I do realize when I need to take a leap of faith and just do it. So, I did the dang thang! I had to do it twice before it all sunk in. Though I cried a lot during the experience, it became the tool that turned on the light inside of me, which I now refer to as the "flashlight of my soul." This heart-wrenching exercise not only transformed my life but also prepared me for my greatest days to come. Traveling back to some of the dark moments granted me the ability to see the light inside of me—and it is bright!

This is what I want for you. I want you to see your light. If you have to go back to some dark places to do it, then do it. Grab your own hand and walk with you. And know this: clear skies come after the rain, and light always peeks out and comes into full view after the darkness.

Lastly, life is made up of multiple seasons. Choose you in every one of them. The blessing of it all is that every season leads to the natural cause and effect of growth or something amazing occurring. The word "season" means a suitable or natural time or occasion. It's a period of the year characterized by a particular circumstance or feature. They are not the same in every part of the world at the same time. Hence, all of it would explain why there is something consistently happening in our lives. Every season in our lives is one that we can learn from. Understanding nature is something that can be very helpful for anyone. Nature runs its course. We don't get to alter it. Our life is the only thing that God has granted us full access to along with the natural things available to us to prosper. But we can't control how our bodies will grow. That's what nature does. We get to participate in it all, and it is vital that we do so. Think about how the earth rotates in its natural function. It does what it does by design. What's amazing is the fact that we can too. The flow of our four seasons is a great tool of inspiration. It is a resource that we can observe and learn from.

Here are some things to take into consideration when it comes to understanding seasons and how they are so in alignment with real life.

Fall is sometimes referred to as "autumn." It's the cooling-off season. Temperatures begin to drop. Most vegetative growth decreases. Animals begin to prepare for the dearth of food that generally comes during the winter by gathering supplies or traveling to warmer climates.

Winter is the time of year when it is very cold. The changes that winter brings affect people, animals, plants, and trees alike. Trees and plants go dormant to live through the cold, and some animals hibernate, while others store up food in the fall to eat during the winter when it gets harder to find food.

Spring comes forth, and the natural world revives and reinvigorates after the colder winter months. This is when seeds take root and vegetation begins to grow.

Summer is the season when temperatures increase to the hottest of the year and may cause droughts for people, animals, and plants.

Do you notice how everything in each season is a preparation for the next one? How cool is that? There is a gathering, changing, growing, and wave effect happening. And don't we all experience these things? In reference to the seasons, how can you benefit from this natural cycle of life?

Here are some questions to reflect on, and I encourage you to be honest with yourself as you read them:

- GATHER – To gather is the process of preparing for completion. What do you need right now? Is there something you need to start or finish? Do you need to save money? Do you need to look for a job? How is your health? Do you need to make a doctor's appointment? Are you taking life notes? What affirmations are you storing up?

- CHANGE – To change is the ability of going in a different direction. It cannot be the same as it was. What can you do differently? Have you considered doing something new? Is there a bad habit you need to stop? Are you ignoring something that keeps coming up for you? Will you take steps that challenge you? What are you afraid of? Are you comfortable? Do you need to move to a different city?

- GROW – To grow is to take action steps necessary for it. Do you take advice? What good seeds are you sowing for your future? Do you need to ignore negativity? Is there something or someone you are waiting on for approval? Are the people in your life helping or hindering you? What good intentions do you make for yourself daily?

The seasons of life can be difficult, but it leaves room for all the ways you can approach each season of your life differently. What you gather and what you change will help you grow. Everything you encounter is all a part of the process and deserves every bit of your time. The journey of depth and discovery is what switches the flashlight of our souls on, and knowing all of you takes a lifetime. Whatever season you are in, enjoy it. You are still here, and there is much for you to do, so make it your only option to live out the "remarkable you."

CHAPTER NINE

NO REGRETS

"Be in this choice, this life, this now."
Nancy Colier

I know a girl from Louisiana who dreamed of being a model. The thought of posing for the camera, wearing beautiful designs, and walking down the runway was just what a small-town girl needed to see her desires come to life. She imagined herself being in the spotlight. Though she had the talent, her dream would end up being a fantasy that got lost in the wind. Without the support and financial resources she needed, those big and bold steps toward a career in this industry seemed impossible for a woman like her. Married to a man who would never consider the possibility of it, and lacking encouragement from her family, she would never take the chance to pursue her dream. It would become a closed chapter before she ever got a chance to see this part written into her life story.

When I heard this story, I was very sad. I can't stand it when women who have big hearts and big dreams never get a chance to see them come to fruition. They age, but they still have that empty space in their hearts. They never fully reach the fulfillment they have longed for all of their lives. Lack of fulfillment and achievement are some of the foundational core issues that birth regret.

Regret is an ongoing crisis in our world. It has a hold on folks like handcuffs. It is best known as sorrow aroused by circumstances beyond one's control or power to repair. The reaction of it is the expression of distress emotionally and mentally. The deep hole of missed opportunities makes it a companion for many.

There are countless stories like the one above. We have family and friends that share this phenomenon. Many women never get to their peak. For some, it seems out of their reach. To this day, I have only met one person in my life that said to me, "I have lived a full life. I am good." When I heard this, I was deeply inspired and thought, *One day I hope those words will come out of my mouth*. Another person who is very close to me somehow knew her days were coming to an end and started preparing all of her loved ones for it. She was completely at peace with the life she had lived. Her surrendered spirit was captivating, because I had been granted access to witness what it looks like to have no regrets. What a remarkable place to be.

We all want this kind of tranquility: a full life with no regrets. Unfortunately, women all over the world have struggled with not knowing how to deal with their ongoing regrets. Since we can't fix them, we ignore them, and therefore they lie dormant in our bodies until something comes to awaken them. And when that happens, the surface feelings of self-doubt, discontentment, misery, and self-pity all come to aid its course.

Regrets come in two forms: the committed and the omitted. The committed regrets are the ones that people put some action to. They actively did something they regret. Many people are in pain over the choices they made and wish they would have done something different. They rehearse over and over how the situation could have been better. If you have ever heard someone say, "I wish I could go back twenty years and correct my mistakes," or "I wish I could take it all back," these are statements of regret.

Omitted regrets are those opportunities people deleted from their life because they didn't have a vision for themselves and so they gave up trying. These people lack faith. They need something tangible in order for them to decide to take a risk. On the other hand, some people make excuses for why they can't do something. You hear them say things like, "I'm too old now, I can't do that," or "I am raising these kids, I don't have time for it." I have even heard folks say, "I don't desire it anymore." Why do people talk themselves out of something they truly wanted? What happened to that desire? Did they get a new dream, or did they let the pain of regret steal their dream? I once spoke with a woman about a beautiful desire that she had. Sometime later, I spoke with her again and she said that God removed it from her heart. In that moment, I felt for her because she did not seem to be happy about it, which got me thinking. Did God move it or did she just give up? I may never know. I personally don't believe that God takes away good, healthy desires. He is a giver, so I can't wrap my brain around that concept. However, I do believe that we as people struggle with doubt and, because of that, we often delete our own desires.

Author Loly Daskal, in one of her blogs titled "12 Things People Regret the Most Before They Die," wrote a list of these regrets. I found it to be very insightful and beneficial. Even at the doorstep of death, regrets haunt the soul. Review the list below and see if you can identify with any of them, or if you have heard someone tell you any of these:

- I wish I had spent more time with the people I love
- I wish I had less worries
- I wish I had forgiven more
- I wish I had stood up for myself
- I wish I had lived my own life
- I wish I had been more honest
- I wish I had worked less
- I wish I had cared less about what other people think
- I wish I had lived up to my full potential
- I wish I had faced my fears
- I wish I had stopped chasing the wrong things
- I wish I had lived more in the moment

It's heartbreaking to know that some have died without getting the opportunities they hoped for. Many of us are right now in this moment, living with a lot of regret that blocks us from living in our now. I don't want you or me to be the ones who come to the place of closing out our last chapter in life with any of the above regrets.

And since we have today, we have a choice in what we will do with our regrets.

One of my biggest regrets is that I never recorded an album. I have been able to perform throughout the US, but I have yet to have a digital catalogue or CD of the original songs I have written. Why haven't I done this for myself? Well, there are a couple of reasons, but I will start with insecurity. I did not think my music was good enough to grace the radio waves. I recorded a couple of singles and barely sold ten. The lack of sales convinced me that I did not have what it takes. Second, I feared the rejection. There are many songwriters out there, and I did not want to compete or have some insensitive and egotistical producer tell me that it didn't sound that great. I had been told that before by one creep; I wasn't going to take a chance on hearing it from another one. Lastly, I had a poor girl's mindset and would entertain many thoughts like, *You don't have the money* and *How are you going to pay for it?* I didn't try to find the money to make it happen. I just believed what my mind told me. I had created a story, and that was my horrible habit.

A regret is a real thing, and it is persuasive. Do you have any regrets? It is very important for all of us to address this issue and do something about it. There is also a myth that I want to dispel, which is that our regrets are because of other people, places, and things. This is not true. We have to terminate these excuses and get personal with ourselves. No one or nothing outside of you can thwart who you are and what you are meant to do. We are all capable individuals who can stand up and face any regret we have.

It is also imperative that we educate ourselves on the nature of regret. Our regrets affect our brain chemistry, and they will continue to grow until we clear the weeds of it. In the reference section of this book, I have included information for you to read more of the scientific research that explains the brain's activity concerning regret. Make sure you take some time to read this, because it will give you some facts about what is going on inside your thought process. Our brain keeps a record of all the activity of who we are; since that is the case, we must take care of ourselves in every way that we can. Don't let regret tell the story of your life. What are you going to do about all the regrets that you have? How do we overcome all of the many "I wishes"? I can only think of one way, which is to be proactive. Start by naming your regret. Go a little deeper and dissect the root of your regret. Is your regret a problem, passion, or purpose?

1. A problem is something that needs solving. Because it's your life, you have the answers, or you can find the answers. Come up with three ways that you can solve this problem. Plan out how you will do it. Pick a date when you will you start the process. For example: If you regret not finishing high school, it's not too late. Maybe you can register for some classes. Or perhaps getting a GED would be sufficient for you.

2. A passion is a strong liking. You want it! It's burning inside of you. What do you have to let go of so that your passion gets fed? Maybe you like sewing, and you want to make outfits for others. How will you do it?

3. Purpose is the reason for which something is done or exists. You are called to do this. No matter what you do, it keeps showing up as the highlight in your life. You're good at it. It's radical, and it even scares you a bit. It may even be challenging because it requires you to

grow. Authenticity is birthed when you take it on. That's purpose, sis. It's waiting on you to partner with your soul. What are you going to do to be in alignment with it?

One of the ways that I was able to overcome a lot of my regrets was to create a habit that would allow me to "ACT" upon a plan for myself. "ACT" is my three-step process that will help you reignite any of your passions that have been cancelled because of your regret.

ACCEPTANCE

There are real feelings, emotions, and memories intertwined with regret. For some of us, there is a lot of pain attached to it, and we may need additional help to heal from it. We must learn how to make peace with our regrets. We start this process with acceptance. Accept that you have regrets. You can no longer view them in a passive way. Many people ignore their reality and try to cover them up by keeping busy with other things that keep them from thinking about it. Approach your regrets with an attitude that communicates your commitment to deal with them.

COMPASSION

Choosing to invest in self-compassion is helpful for your heart. Beating yourself up over what you think you should have done is fruitless. It's a waste of your time and energy and will only deplete you, leaving you empty. You have no power over what was. You only have today. Let yourself off the hook.

My therapist once quoted this statement, which I agree with: "Humans have never been perfect." We need to stop trying to hold on to what inevitably is not in our control.

TRANSITION

Leave the old behind and step into a new direction. What do you really want to work on in your life? Choose one thing that matters to you. Change your perspective, if need be. Take a leap of faith with action. Brainstorm new ways that will help you reach new goals. Change your language from "I wish" to "I will." Take a risk! If something doesn't work out, focus on learning from it. If something does work out, it is your victory, so celebrate it.

After you have done the above, go to the nearest mirror and say, "Girllll, you did it. I knew you would." Next, share the victory by telling a friend what you did for yourself.

In closing, psychotherapist Nancy Colier states that there is no choice that is a wrong choice. She says: "Be in this choice, this life, this now and stop imagining that reality could be or could have been anything other than what it is." I love this quote because it inspires me to stay present in all that I do. It's time to cancel your regret subscription. You do not need it, so do not let it take up any more of your precious time and energy. Give yourself permission to turn in a new direction and decide what you want your life to be on the other side of your regret.

CHAPTER TEN

OWN YOUR LIFE

"Love yourself first and everything else falls in line.
You really have to love yourself
to get anything done in this world."
Lucille Ball

When you know who you are, you will let nothing get in the way of owning the life you are blessed to have. Ownership is something that people desire to have in their lives, but the challenge is that many of us don't own our lives. God, who is sovereign over all things, has given us the power to take ownership of our lives, yet it is one of the hardest things for us to do. The concept of ownership is understanding that you have the responsibility for your life. There are no other individuals who are responsible for the life you have and the way you will live it. As an adult, YOU are your person. This does not mean that you don't need people in your life; it simply means that they are not the decision-makers or the responsibility-takers for you. If you embrace this truth, this means you will get all of you—no regrets, no leftovers, no substitutes, just being you.

Sometimes life can become so stressful, but you must zoom in and take a closer look to see how to be a great steward. One of the ways that we hinder our own progress is when we do too many things. It tends to create a life overload, and it feels like a pot of hot stew: many things brewing all at one time. Though we are gifted individuals, we haven't quite figured out how to stay in the lane that leads us to our best work. When you take inventory of your life, you will become so aware of your needs and see yourself clearly.

I love a great stew, but when it is missing a few ingredients, my tastebuds can tell the difference. What about you? Do you like stew? Stews usually have very specific ingredients that make them taste the way they do. Can you tell the difference when your favorite stew does not taste the same? In such cases, you might not want to eat it, or, if you are creative, you will add something to make it better. Life can often resemble a pot of stew. It could have a lot of ingredients or be in need of some extra seasoning.

We are all facing different seasons in our lives and are reflecting on our youthful years. Some of us are thinking about our relationships and trying to decide what's next for us, while others are stuck and don't know what we are supposed to do with the rest of our lives. Any of these feelings can make a person feel incomplete and unfulfilled. We don't like this truth, but it is what it is.

There were many times in my life when I did not have ownership. In fact, I never even thought of it or asked myself this question. My life was attached to all the things I was doing and the people I was doing them with. One of the biggest revelations in my life was when I realized that a lot of folks owned pieces of my life. I want to get deep down to the nitty-gritty with what I am about to say, because I want to be one hundred with you. As a Christian woman, my desire is to honor God with the life he has blessed me with. However, my walk with the Lord got very cloudy at one point. Though I made Jesus Lord of my life many years ago, it became very clear to me one day that He did not have that role at all times. My heart was to follow him, obey his Word, and follow the leaders in my life. I put my best foot forward. I didn't want anything questionable or left undone. But there is another side to this story that I want you to be aware of, so I am going to give you a few details in hopes that I may shine a light into my situation. Y'all know that every relationship has some difficulties. It ain't always filled with rose petals and daisies. Sometimes it's thorns and dried-up leaves.

For many years, me and the Lord were solid, until he revealed to me that there was a problem in our relationship. What happened for me was that I became so focused on pleasing my leaders that I lost sight of God's directives in my life. I started to look to my leaders for how I was going to do life. That meant unless they okayed it, I wasn't doing it. Or if they said to do it, I'd do it thinking that I was doing the right thing. I was so dedicated to the leaders, church, and the system of the church that I attached all of this to my relationship with God. It was great to have a church community that I could grow with spiritually and leaders who could help me in the process. I was very dedicated to what I thought the formula of honoring God was supposed to look like. It is good to obey your leaders, because the scriptures teach this principle. However, the scriptures will never teach you to dismiss the Holy Spirit. Unfortunately, other voices were more prominent than God's voice. This was unhealthy and unholy.

Giving up your soul to people is one of the most devastating things you can do. It will leave you spiritually dry. They don't have ownership over your life. But that is what I had given my church and its leaders. If you are not able to look at God's Word for yourself and place your allegiance there, then you can potentially be misled and end up confused. I did not have spiritual balance in my life. The way I was living was under, for, and through them. This was how I functioned for a very long time in my life. They were my prepositions. Being that a preposition is an act of preposing or placing before or in front of something else, I was under their influence. I waited for people to tell me how and when to live my life. I struggled to make basic decisions for myself, like what class I should take in school, when I should take vacation for myself, or even trying to decide what picture I would post on my social media pages. I would ask people to give me their input on the simplest things. I was not confident in my own choices. I became resentful and had many regrets, and it was all on me. No one ever forced me to do anything. I gave my choices away when I agreed to things that did not sit right with my conscious.

This is how you know when you don't own your life. Anything that violates your inner and outer being is an automatic NO. In all honesty, I had placed others in front of myself and God, and therefore I lacked ownership of my life. I am spilling the tea now because I had to clean up my own mess, and you may need to do the same for yourself.

This kind of giving up of yourself for others is a huge

crisis. It is what leaves people with a hole in their heart. It is not only happening in the church but also in other areas of life. We face this in our jobs, in our relationships, families, organizations, groups, and the like. There are people in your life who are little mini-gods, and they should not have that spot because they were not created for it. Leaders are in a position for a reason and a season, but we must never make them a lord over our lives. I got it twisted, and I had to learn from my mistakes. What I learned is that I had some idol worship going on. Their words became so loud that I thought I could not hear God personally unless it was through them. Something we must all come to realize is that it's not God, them, and then you. The proper channel is God, you, and then others. Your spirit will always clarify things that are not in rhythm with truth. Anytime you have to get someone else to clarify or confirm you or your choice, it's clearly codependency and a lack of ownership. My priorities had to be reset, and I had to create a new way of doing life.

Just like stew with half the ingredients is not going to fulfill your tastebuds, your life should not lack the ingredients you need to live it. This means you will have to own all of it. If you are getting this message and you know you need help, this next part is for you big time. In order for you to own your life, you have to focus on your greater purpose, and this will require you to ask yourself more questions. Why is it important to own your life? What is in the way of you taking ownership of your life? Give yourself some time to reflect a bit and then write down your thoughts. None of us has fully arrived with all the answers to life, but we can start with what we do know.

In my lifetime, if there is anything that I have learned

that is very important for me to share, it is the ability to create life hacks that have guided me to personally own my life. I want to take you on the journey of building your own "*life recipe*." This way you will know what to put in and what to leave out. There are three things that we must be careful and cautious with, and those are influence, idolatry, and your own independence.

> INFLUENCE is the ability to have an effect on the character, development, or behavior of someone or something. It can be empowering, but when a person disregards imitation and chooses duplication, it is toxic.

> IDOLATRY is the worship of idols. It is extreme admiration, love, and reverence for something or someone. People and things can be loved, but anything that becomes an obsession leads to chaos.

> INDEPENDENCE is the fact or state of being independent. This is the ingredient that grants you the power to own your own life, but you must be aware of its alter ego. Remember who created you; you have a higher power to yield to.

All three of these can be stumbling blocks. They all have an underlying layer of deceit. You don't have to participate with their deceptive ways, but you can learn from them.

These can also be a barometer to alert your awareness. I want to highlight a specific way that people get robbed in life by influence and idolatry. It is when they look at all of the people around them who appear to be thriving and feel depressed watching them. I tell my daughter all the time to get off social media watching other people's lives and start building her own life. I hope she listens to me one day. The countless hours we put into watching our likes and the lack thereof could be used instead to build our life and go to our next level. Every second that we waste is one that we could be using to nourish ourselves. You cannot get time back. It's impossible.

Side bar: Y'all, a lot of the stuff you see on the internet is a lot of hogwash. Some of it is staged and is a false presentation of truth. It's completely inauthentic. You don't know what these people really do. And, to be honest, it's really not any of your concern how great someone is doing unless you want to support and cheer them on. Other than that, keep it moving and don't fall for the hype. Instead of looking at someone else's life for verification of what your life should look like, focus on cultivating your own. Imagine what you could accomplish by investing time in you rather than indulging and entertaining things that do not give back to you.

Every individual must come to the realization that it is a blessing to have ownership of their life rather than being a wandering soul. When you see yourself as a person able to manage and take care of YOU fully, it is empowering. It has been wonderful and exciting to step up and take on the role of owning my own life, and I know that you want to do the same thing for yourself. The recipe for owning your life requires you to add some necessary ingredients that will enhance your ability to take ownership: they are responsibility, righteousness, and resilience.

RESPONSIBILITY longs for the soul to embrace it. It is one of the most effective first steps that I made for myself. When a person does not take responsibility for their own actions and choices, they will live in a state of denial. Responsibility says "I own my stuff." It acknowledges mistakes and prepares for the mission of growth. When you take it on, you will have no regrets and will be able to see the possibilities ahead of you.

RIGHTEOUSNESS craves all of your attention and abilities. It is saying "I will do what I know is right. I will not settle for mediocre living." It's bold and believes in all the good there is to experience. There is no negotiation with righteousness, because it strives for excellence.

RESILIENCE embodies overcoming. It is fully aware of all that you have been through in your life but lives with hope. There is a strong, determined spirit in resilience. It is confident and courageous enough to leap forward. It believes that it will achieve all that it desires. Resilience knows that it's a winner and always finishes what it started.

These are the essentials for anyone willing and ready to walk faithfully into ownership. Think about it this way: If you owned a car, would you ignore putting gas in it when needed? Would you let the antifreeze run out? The answer is no, because you want that car to keep running for as long as it can. You'd make sure there was gas in it and that the engine was serviced. The mechanic is your friend, because you trust that your needs will be taken care of.

Spiritually speaking, God is my mechanic. He fixes all of my broken parts and services the parts that need maintenance. I know that he has given me complete ownership, but as an owner, I know that I am need to go to the mechanic. Just like a car, the engine will break down if the owner does not take care of it. As a human, the engine, which I will refer to as our soul, is desperately in need of constant care. If we don't nurture ourselves, we will find ourselves in the condition of an engine that doesn't work any longer.

I had to build on this core principle of taking care of myself. I have practiced the above steps, and let me just tell you, they have transformed my life. It is the simple things you do that will make a huge difference. When you practice ownership of your life, you will see the kind of growth that extends itself out to blessing others.

I will leave you with a few basic things that you can do on a regular basis that will keep you focused on owning your life:

DO SOMETHING FOR YOU: Go on a thirty-minute walk at least three times a week. It will rejuvenate you, replenish your spirit, and help realign you with your goals and intentions. It decreases stress and allows you to be free to hear all the things around you.

DO SOMETHING NEW: Reading a new book can open up the heart and mind to consider new things. Playing a new game creates an energy flow that brings out the fun in you. Taking a weekly bubble bath will pamper every part of you.

DO NOTHING: Practice being still. Turn off all the sounds around you. This includes your phone. Your body wants to communicate with you. Your mind, body, and soul crave full connection. Stop whatever you are doing for seven minutes of silence.

This last one was the hardest for me, because I can

be a busy bee. My mind usually works at a fast pace. I often have to slow down and enjoy a moment of nothingness. Let me tell you, this will be extremely beneficial so you can be and stay present with what is happening in your life and around you.

Preparation for your next season is a must for those who take ownership. Take responsibility for where your life is now. Let righteousness fuel you. Be the kind of person who wants to be all that you can be. Don't ever settle for a substitute version of yourself. Be resilient; it is the part of you that demonstrates your ability to persevere.

You have pressed and pushed through many things. God gave you all that you need so that you can live an amazing and beautiful life. So, always strive to succeed in your life: acknowledge your needs, celebrate your accomplishments, and take action daily.

CHAPTER ELEVEN

RHYTHM AND STRIDE

"Not even me can stop me."
Jennifer Lewis

Are you a music lover? Music has brought so much joy to people all over the world. It's so cool when you hear a song that gets all up in your body and you start to rock your head from side to side while tapping your feet to the beat. The sound travels throughout your body, and every part of you is in rhythm. There is a classic groove by Lisa Lisa & Cult Jam called "Let the Beat Hit 'Em" that reminds me of the effect that music has on us. It makes us want to dance and sing. But when the music stops, the energy within us shifts, our flow is interrupted, and the beat within us comes to an end.

Like music, our life flow has a rhythm and a stride to it. It's the part of us that will either give us our best song or reveal an inner fluctuation gone wrong. Have you ever heard the saying, "They hit their stride"? This sounds like someone finally made progress or hit their target. I have heard all kinds of old sayings and quotes over the years. I had no idea what folks were talking about with most of them, but this one I get it. It's the journey of the one who owns their life and has a rhythm that propels them to walk in stride. It's character that reflects growth and a confidence that dismisses any form of an ego. This is the moment when everything in your life has an authentic beat that is unstoppable. It's the anthem that you can declare like Jennifer Lewis said in an interview, "Not even me can stop me." Y'all, when I heard this, I knew these words were meant for me too. The message was so loud and clear. This is a woman who has a rhythm and stride that she has nurtured and is committed to living it out in every aspect of her life to the fullest.

How can we all master such conviction? What would this look like if we had this attitude? Who can stop me? When you realize that you must be so bold and courageous with yourself, you will be determined to win, and building your own rhythm and stride is essential to doing so.

RHYTHM

Rhythm is the essence of music. It's when two or more beats are organized into a pattern across a length of time, forming a rhythm. Metaphorically, a rhythm is what our bodies experience with our everyday lives. It is based on how you normally do things and the patterns you have created. It is repetitive in nature. It may change only to accommodate what your plans are for the day. For example, if you go to work daily or take your kids to school, this is your rhythm. It is something that you are accustomed to. There is not a lot of thought put into it; you just do it. Whether it is fast or slow, the beat is within your command. Every second, minute, or hour relies on you to manage it.

STRIDE

A stride is moving with or as if with long steps. It's the natural pace—maximum competence or capability. It's a stage of progress. This is the part of your life that takes more effort. Though it has a natural flow, you will have to move with it in order to keep it. If you change, it will change. A stride is when you take steps in a specific direction, knowing where you want to go. Think of a runner. They know what they have to do to cross that finish line. I believe some runners don't worry about who they have to beat because their focus is greater. Their sight is on what is ahead. This is why when some athletes don't win, they are not discouraged. Crossing the finish line was their successful accomplishment, and sometimes that is enough for them. The requirement, however, is to give all of your ability. There is no half-steppin' when it comes to a stride. It demands all of you.

This year has been an exciting journey for me, but it has not come without a few bumps, bruises, and some scars—emotionally, that is. I discovered that I struggle with depression. I had a hard time accepting this because I had a false concept of depression. I thought that it would ruin me and I was actually scared of it. I did not like the mental or physical exhaustion I was experiencing in my life because of it but I had to embrace it in order to take care of me.

Just this past week I had an experience of depression where I felt sad, low energy, and had no motivation to do much of anything. Prior to this, I had been on an upward trajectory, but the winds of life came and blew me off course, from marriage challenges, planning to relocate to another state, and building a business that just doesn't seem to be getting off the ground. After a year of putting all of my energy into my business, it did not reach any of the goals that I had in mind. I laid in my bed stiffly, almost unable to move. It was the tension in my body that had a hold on me. When I got on a virtual call with my marriage therapist, I started to talk, but I couldn't help but cry in the midst of it. I was feeling some strong emotions regarding my life. Because I was so focused on taking care of many other things, I did not take the time to examine what was going on inside of me. Usually, I am able to spot when something is off, but this time it was different. No matter what I did, nothing changed the feeling. I was out of rhythm, and my stride was faulty.

As I write these words in this moment, I would like to tell you how amazing I am doing now, but to be honest, this is a new level of discovery or, shall I say, acknowledgment. I have felt these feelings before, but I had never given them the full attention they needed. But now, I am alert and attentive and making some healthy choices for myself. I will not let depression rule me. It has become a huge indicator for me to know when my rhythm and stride have been sidetracked.

What is it for you? How do you identify what is affecting your life? Do you have any warning signs? What different emotions show up? All the work that you have done up to this point is so good, and I want you to stay the course. Developing and maintaining a solid rhythm and stride will help you thrive through the challenges and hardships that happen in life. It allows you the flexibility and freedom to move at your pace. Your way will be completely different from mine. However, we both are in need of living life in rhythm and a stride. Don't cheat on this one because it cannot be negotiated. When you're in stride, your life moves with intention and fluidity.

The first thing you must do is investigate what is and what is not in order in your life. Let me explain what it means to be out of order. When life is overwhelming, neglected, or chaotic, it means that something is out of order. If there is even a hint of disruption from the natural human tendency that craves structure, you can be sure that something is on shaky grounds. For example, if you have a huge load of laundry in your home that is piling up and your washing machine is broken, you will not be able to wash your clothes because it is out of order. You can go to the laundromat, but that adds an extra thing to your schedule. And who wants an extra thing? It is the same way with your life. If something is not working for you, then it is out of order and may need some adjustments or repair.

Most of my life, I have been a busy chick. There were times I was doing so much I couldn't keep up with me. My rhythm and stride at times were nonexistent. I settled for a cheap version of myself. I was so overwhelmed and, let me just tell you, it was obvious in the way I spoke to others and the way it was visually present in my eyes and on my body. Ladies, that's where it will reflect the most. When people asked me how I was doing, I would say those famous words, "I'm fine." This was a bad habit of mine until I learned a better way.

Have you ever said that, knowing you were *not* fine? Here is the deal: folks know when you are not telling the truth. When exhaustion is visible all over you, you can't hide. So, there is no need to pretend like you are okay.

Just tell the truth and walk in your reality. Start identifying what is getting in the way of you not being fine. Get skilled at knowing what is out of order in your life. Then give yourself a talk and tell YOU that you are not settling for less.

Below are some indicators to help evaluate the structure of your life and whether you have a rhythm and stride or if it may be in need of a tune-up.

- Are you a busy person?
- How much time do you spend on social media?
- What do you say no to? Or do you ever say no?
- What do you do for yourself on a weekly basis? (Example: weekly massage)
- Over twenty-four hours, how much water do you drink?
- When was the last time you made a phone call to someone you love?
- Do you invest in yourself (treating yourself to dinner, or taking a self-development program)?

You should be able to answer the above questions in about thirty seconds if you know yourself well. If you second-guess it or have to backtrack to figure it out, then you need to turn yourself in, sis.

I typically check in with myself when I am out of balance. I start with a who, what, and how self-questionnaire. So, who is reading this book right now? Go ahead, say it out loud. This is not a trick question. YOU are reading this book, so that is your who. This is a simple way to get you to connect with yourself and to make it personal. When things get personal, they become important. Who gets to do this work? Who will decide how it is done? Who will be responsible for finishing it? Oh, and for the record, no one else gets to be involved with this process—not your husband, kids, or friends. So don't even think of asking them for any advice about your who, what, and how. It's all on you.

Next, what are you going to do for yourself? What commitment will you make in order to participate in this exercise? What will you put in place, and what will you eliminate? Then, how will you create it? How much time do you need? How do you know what it will look like? Make sure you write all of your answers down, because this is the template for creating a healthy rhythm and stride. Reference and reflect on it daily. As you continue to learn more about you, build upon it.

Lastly, create a mantra that makes a statement about you. What do you want to say about yourself, and what do you want to be known for? This is one of the best ways you can demonstrate how much you love you. When your rhythm and stride reflect the life you want to live, nothing will be able to stop you.

CHAPTER TWELVE

PRACTICE PURPOSE

"Live the life you were born for."

One of the most amazing things for every human being is to understand that everything they go through in life leads to something, and that is PURPOSE.

What actually is purpose? I believe purpose is that thing you were born for. It's the calling of your entire being. It's the reason God made you. No one is born without one, and everyone is in need of seeking and finding it. It's the meaning of your life. Once you take ownership of your life, you are in the prime position for living in your purpose. The power and value of this type of lifestyle is the anchor to the soul. Since purpose is the *big* life plan for every person on the earth, it would benefit us all to practice it over and over until it is our way of life. If every person on the earth understood their purpose, there would be way more change. Communities would be stronger, and the division in our world would find its way to global unity. When we don't live in our purpose, we actually resist growth and live deterred and delayed lives. There is nothing better for you than to live in, for, and through your purpose.

There are people who are so clear about what God has called them to do, and it is beautiful to watch them in action. They have deep convictions and are confident. When they walk into a room, people take notice, because their aura glows fully. They possess a magnetic draw that sets the tone. Have you ever noticed when a person speaks and you can hear the passion in their purpose without them ever saying exactly what it is? It's so powerful to watch the excitement coming out of their body.

But some people are not sure what they are meant to do and why they are here. They need a little help to understand how to find their purpose. Then there is another group of individuals who are the in-betweens. They may feel an inkling, but they ignore it. There is a tugging on their heart, directing them into position to unleash it, but they keep telling themselves that they will get around to it. To this day, it is still waiting for them to make a move. These are the people who have chosen to live life neglecting the full human experience. In such cases, there is a resistance to launch. Others push it away because they don't want the pressure of having to be on the front line of possible failure or ridicule. They know something is supposed to change in their life, but they won't go for it. And there are some folks who don't want to acknowledge it at all because committing to it would mean they would have to grow up and do something with their lives.

Everything I have shared with you in this book is designed to give you that extra push to live your life 100 percent. This last part is one of the most challenging subjects that could get in the way of all that I have mentioned so far. Fear and procrastination are two very big reasons why ignoring and resistance have dug their heels in peoples' lives, literally holding them down.

PROCRASTINATION

The etymology of procrastination in Latin is *procrastinare*. It means "to forward to the next day." I don't like procrastination. It makes me so mad because it haunts us and fights against everything good we set out to do. I want you to get indignant with me about this 'cause this is serious stuff. This ugly devil is like a knife that cuts and causes people to bleed out spiritually. It is a liar that talks big and tricks you into believing you can postpone, reschedule, and wait till tomorrow. Sis, honestly? You don't have tomorrow. Don't listen to it. This sneaky thing wants to sabotage every step you make. We should never delay what we could do today.

When you procrastinate, you sign up to a quitting mentality. "Quitter" loves wearing folks down so that they will give up. All who are under its influence must come to realize that quitters never win and winners never quit. Knowing the strategy of procrastination and what it is capable of is vital. It seeks to stifle your capacity to be effective and productive. This little enemy is on a mission to suffocate the greatness that is in you. So please be aware as you take steps to live in purpose. "Quitter" and Procrastination will not stop until they have taken you through their own elimination process to destroy your purpose.

FEAR

Fear is an unpleasant feeling triggered by the perception of danger, real or imagined. Imagination can be a wonderful experience when the mind wonders at amazing things. However, if the mind imagines what is false or negative, it becomes dark and twisted. Fear loves to keep people in the dark; that is where it does its dirty work. It demolishes character and is the silent killer that enjoys slaying all who live by it. When people let fear dictate their life, they are only experiencing bits and pieces of real living. It is impossible to live out the best version of yourself when you are fearful. It is an insult to the soul to give only half of you to this life you are living. This is why you must be alert and connect with yourself so deeply that you do not let anything distract you from practicing your purpose daily.

These two imposters attacked my life and held me hostage for years. Truth be told, they did get the best of me until I stood up to them. I developed three p's that help me think about my own challenges and how to be vigilant when dealing with procrastination and fear.

PURPOSE PERPETRATORS

A perpetrator is very deceptive, and it intends to carry out a harmful act. Fear and procrastination are ready to harm you. They paralyze people and hinder their growth and purpose.

Start confronting them. Let these perpetrators know that you are not participating with them. When you feel like putting off what you need to get done, remind yourself that you will finish what you started. Later is too late. Get it done now.

PURPOSE PROSECUTORS

These are the ones that try to convince you that you don't have what it takes to win in life. They like to make claims against you. These bullies will infiltrate your life and leave you with a lack of joy, frustration, complaining, ingratitude, indecisiveness, codependency, negative thinking, irritation, jealousy, envy, being unorganized, inconsistency, lack of discipline, lack of responsibility, carelessness, comparing your life with others, people pleasing, doing things to be noticed, wanting others' approval, dishonesty with self, and a lack of self-worth. It seeks to convict you to a life sentence of failure. But that is not what you are, because you are a woman who follows through and handles your business. Your best defense against the prosecutor is to be your best evidence.

PURPOSE PURSUERS

People who live in their purpose have chosen to settle for nothing less. They don't take shortcuts. They don't let imposters come in and take them off course. They are focused, steady, moving in rhythm, and passionately pursuing their purpose unapologetically. Many of them understand there is something greater than themselves. Their stillness is only yielded to God, who is their greater source. They are the kind of people who go all the way, because they know that to live in purpose is what gives their lives meaning. They push through all the obstacles, because purpose is priority.

When I discovered that I wasn't living out my purpose, it was humbling, but I knew that I had to get focused on what was important to me. I remember having so many areas of my life off-balance. Like when I took a job knowing that it didn't pay what I was worth, thinking that it would get me in the door for something else. Y'all, there was no other door. I invented this scenario because it justified me taking the job. I wanted the job because I wanted to be active doing something.

I never like being still, because if I am not moving and grooving, shaking and baking up something amazing, then life is boring. I have to be doing something. I don't have time to rest. One of my family members told me a long time ago that you rest when you go to heaven. So, I kinda kept that in the back of my mind, and it became a mindset mantra for keeping busy. Who wants to go to heaven exhausted? Not me, but if you knew me then, you'd think I enjoyed chasing exhaustion. After all, I was making the world better, right? I was saving lives. Let me correct my crazy! I don't save lives; Jesus does that. I assist people with their lives, so let me make sure I tell the truth. I thought I was doing something mighty when I was actually living below my standards and was not practicing living in my purpose. I had settled for a fake version of it. That job never turned into anything better for me.

Another thing I would do is get involved in projects or volunteer my services for free because I could do it and I am actually gifted at it. Or I would serve because, as a disciple of Jesus, that's what I'm supposed to do. All of this can be good, but when it is not done with purpose in mind, it's unhealthy.

Some of us have so many talents, there is not much you *can't* do. The challenge is when we try to use all of our talents at the same time. For example, I have a background in event management. I could run a theater production from top to bottom—hire the cast, book the room, run the rehearsals, send out the emails, schedule the production, and tell everybody how the day is going to go. I can do that easily, but do I love it? Heck no! I enjoy being the artist in the production. I am a storyteller. The stage is my playground, and I love to play. But there have been a few occasions where I took on a task to run a production when I should have declined, because it was not my purpose. All of this taught me a valuable lesson. I learned that if what I am doing does not match my value system, I can't do it. I literally have to say NO. If it doesn't have PURPOSE on the top, the bottom, in the middle, and wrapped around it, then it's not for me. It took me a long time to get good at this.

It's not that difficult to find your purpose, because you already have it deep within you. However, please be aware that just because you can do a job or task well doesn't mean it's your purpose. It just means that God has blessed you with some extra skills. You have to get aligned with the throughline in your life. What is that recurring thing that continues to show up? Pay attention to when you do something over and over again. It's going to either galvanize you and you want to do it more, or it's going to exhaust you, leaving you with the aftereffects of a purpose prosecutor. That primary thing that you are supposed to be doing is where focus, energy, and faith are completely aligned. I had to go on this same journey and spend time with my creator so that I could get confirmation as to where he was leading me. I desperately needed wisdom so I could fully understand how to practice purposeful living. So, I had to inquire of God by reading scripture. James 1:5 (ESV) says, "If any of you lacks wisdom, let him ask God, who gives generously to all without reproach, and it will be given him." And let me tell you, this is a never-ending practice for me. Living out your purpose is not a one-time conversation with God. It's a lifetime conversation. And you will have to choose it daily.

All of us will have to come face-to-face with why and what we are here for. Every day that you have is a day that you can live out your purpose. Every year we get to be here will require a re-evaluation and an adjustment. It's as simple as understanding what you can still do, what you cannot do, and what you will do. If you are thirty years old, the things that you did in your twenties are considered your past. Because you are at a different place in your life, those things may not help you now. I am not referring to those golden and wise directives that your parents or someone very special in your life gave you. I am talking about things like if you used to go to the bar every weekend and now you have to do prep work before you go to the office on Monday at 8 a.m., you probably are not doing that as much. If you are still trying to live like you did ten years ago, then you are not living life in reality.

Change is inevitable. Studies show that there is a natural progression that takes place through every age demographic. This requires us to make some adjustments in order to continue to live purpose-filled lives. Nuffield Health did an article that says there are six different stages of a woman's life. Through every stage, purpose must be present.

LIFE STAGES

Stage 1: Young Women – From a girl to a young woman. Changes in your body in every area. Your brain is growing strong. You are curious and ready to experience life. It's the "I can do anything" stage.

Stage 2: Career, Family, Fun – It's the peak season! Many women want to settle down and have a family.

Entrepreneurship is on the radar. Lots of creativity is birthed. People are enjoying their lives.

Stage 3: Life Balance – Middle-aged women who have had some great success. They are rediscovering new ways of doing things. Their parents are getting older and need them. They need balance in their lives. Self-care is a priority.

Stage 4: Back to You – The milestone life. These women are experiencing changes emotionally, mentally, and physically. Menopause has come to visit. They are dedicated to living their next years intentionally. They are taking time to nurture their souls. Some are exploring a new dream or hobby.

Stage 5: Freedom to Explore – Retirement on the horizon. The daily routine will be different than before. The possibilities are exciting. It's the "What do I want to do next?" phase.

Stage 6: Experienced, Thankful, Content – They have lived, loved, and laughed. It's the moment when you can say, "I have lived a good life."

The biggest thing all of the stages above have in common is that we are all getting older, and life is going to move forward whether any of us want to participate or not. Every human being must participate in their own life in order to see its full potential. Not everyone lives long enough to experience every stage, but the amazing part is that each one offers something remarkable to look forward to. When you focus on practicing purpose, you take every stage and make it work for you. According to Nuffied Health, our psychological well-being peaks at about age eighty-two. When I read that, I was like, "Lord, let me get to that peak." I am coming for you, number eighty-two and beyond. I love these stages, because it actually helps me to live my life in real time and not force anything. I am free to be me.

So, sis, take a deep breath and relax. This removes the pressure of having to be on point every day, all day, all the time. It's okay when you don't have everything in perfect order on a given day. My hope for you is to be present in your life, not perfect. You are allowed a pause so that you can make the necessary changes you need.

I hope that everything you have learned from the previous chapters serves you and helps guide you to reflect, take care of yourself, and be your best YOU. The world has put a lot of pressure on all of us with its false standards of what our lives should be and what our level ups should look like. But in reality, it is the standards that you are creating for yourself that will help you live your life well. It's about having boundaries that protect you from all of the useless junk that comes your way. When you know you well, you will eliminate anything from your life that doesn't support you or help you practice purpose.

One of the most misleading ideas that deter people from their purpose is convincing them to participate in many things that appear to be legit opportunities. There is a spiritual epidemic that I believe is crippling people, and that is the practice of getting the bag and having ten or more different streams of income in order to get it. I get really ticked off when I hear people teach the hustling principle with a manipulative mission. This concept does not help you with your character or teach you how to truly align yourself with your purpose. It's all about what you can get and how to have all these things. This can get tricky, because what works for them may not work for you. Here is the scoop: if hustling is the equivalent of being a hardworking individual then, yes, I can get down with that. But if hustling is getting ahead by any means necessary, check it, because you don't have time to get caught up in what is not leading you to your purpose.

In any given case, always ask yourself: What are you hustling for? Why is it important? How does it make you better? Pursuing many different things all at one time is the number one way to keep a person distracted from their God-given calling. It throws you off track and will keep you deceived. It strips you of your ability to make good decisions. It looks good in your twenties, because in the younger years, you are ready to take on the world. You are building the dream. We all want the bag, but we better get really clear about the bags that will be under our eyes in our forties, fifties, and up. There are so many delayed side effects from the hustle: digestive problems, liver dysfunction, cortisol overflow, hormonal challenges, cloudy minds, and a frustrated spirit, just to name a few.

A hustle can be like multitasking. Women have been able to do some great things over the years. We have amazing skills and incredible qualities, but it is not wise to multitask. Multitasking has been known to decrease your focus and can cause harm to the brain. You need to be able to concentrate on one thing, do it well, and then teach somebody else. If you want to keep up with the Joneses, then go ahead and pursue many avenues. But if you lose you in the process, then what was it all for?

There are twenty-four hours in a day. If you break it down, there are 1,440 minutes total. Keep in mind, seven or more of those hours need to be for sleep. So, you really only have seventeen flexible hours, which is 1,020 minutes to work with. Use these minutes wisely. You can split your time, but do not split your mind. Y'all, I did all of the things that I thought would bless me, but it actually blocked me. Because I was multitasking and hustling on a daily basis, I hardly got any sleep. I ended up with insomnia, which wrecked my life big time. I can't say this enough: life has a natural rhythm, and anything that goes against yours will ultimately lead you to crash and burn. So don't get caught up in what appears to be the norm. Your normal will look different from everybody else's. Focus on practicing your purpose, not hustling and dying trying.

Practicing your purpose is a necessity, and you will have to continue asking yourself the right questions that lead you to it or leverage your way in it. Some good ones to start with are: Is there something that God keeps showing me? What subject matter excites and ignites me? What do I enjoy? Do I have fun at it? Does it challenge or grow me? These help you stay in tune with your gifts and abilities so that you are not misled to do things that are not divinely designed for you. For example, if someone asks you to do something, think it through first. If you are unclear, ask more questions that help you figure out whether you can do the job or not. Ask yourself: Do I want to do this? Does it align with my skills? How much time will this take me? Will my contributions make a difference? This process will give you some answers to work with. People will respect your honesty and integrity when you respond with your yes or no from the place of living in purpose.

As we come to a landing with this final chapter, this last practical tool will encapsulate this journey you have been on with me. It is what I call a "LIFE MODULE," also known as "LIFEMOD." With all the work I have done for myself, this one practice I learned has benefited me in so many ways. I would like for you to make one for yourself, take a picture of it, and put it where you will always have access to it.

A module is a standard or unit of measurement. Because your life deserves a standard for how you practice purpose, you need to be able to measure your progress. The rhythm and stride chapter helps you create steps for healthy living, and the life module is the standard for how you will live out those steps. Let me tell you what a life module includes, but first you must know that every human being will have a different one. A LIFEMOD includes anything that you do all the time that builds your life. In fact, it's a real representation of the shape of your life. It is the non-negotiables that you can't live without. For an example, here is my personal course breakdown for my own LIFEMOD.

Module 1: **L** - Live well: I spend time with God daily reading my Bible or going on a prayer walk. It is important for me to eat healthy, exercise, drink lots of water, do self/soul-care, be creative, and take a sabbath day

Module 2: **I** – Intentional Investment: My family are the first people to get all of my love. It's my decision to date my spouse and to connect with my mom and daughters by doing things with them that build our relationship. This is my necessity.

Module 3: **F** – <u>Focus power:</u> I spend time learning new things and using my gifts through entrepreneurship, leadership, creativity, and performing. I seek to inspire and empower women toward personal and spiritual growth.

Module 4: **E** – <u>Engagement:</u> My community is a resource that I value. Spending time with friends, doing Bible study, corporate worship, supporting others, and partnering with like-minded people are essential.

Module 5: **M** – <u>Management:</u> Take notice of what is out of order. Making sure that I don't overdo anything but instead live balanced. This also includes my financial habits, like budgeting and not overspending.

Module 6: **O** – <u>Observation:</u> I look at the needs around me, and I get involved, like giving to the church and donating to charitable organizations. I also coach, cultivate new practices, and create new opportunities.

Module 7: **D** – <u>Determination:</u> Before I go to bed at night, I pray, clear my head, and let go of anything that does not need to go to sleep with me or carry into my tomorrow.

This is something that I have practiced doing for a very long time. I don't waver, because I am committed to my own personal growth and the life that I have chosen to live. Most of these modules are daily, while others are planned for a future time. However, any of them will give me a clear measure of how I am doing in my life and if I am practicing my purpose.

Whatever you do daily can be a part of your life module. There is no right or wrong way, because it's based on your individual life. Second, zoom in on what benefits you and what does not. Consider whether what you are doing is working or not. You should never feel stress, anxiety, or confusion over anything you write down for yourself. Anything that is not working should not be a part of your life module. Perhaps you need to change something to get it in alignment with your life or get rid of it. It is soaking up good energy, and you need all of YOU to excel.

Lastly, think about where you are going. What do you want to complete in the next thirty days? After that, move forward and make yourself a ninety-day completion plan, then six months to a year and beyond. Look at the stages of life to help you with this process. Start with three to six things that will allow you to measure what you do consistently. The purpose of this is to keep you in movement to practice your purpose. Please also understand that there are new things that you will need to add and cultivate so that you will master this process. You also may have a moment of revelation as you do this. When these sparkle moments happen, have fun with them.

As you get older, adjustments will continually need to be made to assist you in your season of life. My life module goes with me wherever I go, and I apply it in whatever I do. If any area of my life is neglected in any way, then I know clearly that there is something going on with me. It allows me the opportunity of checking in with myself. In such times, I go back and re-evaluate my steps and take care of my business. Much of what I've talked about in this book is the process of being committed and consistent in caring for your total self.

When you truly understand your value, you will not settle for anything less than the best offer of yourself.

Our opportunities are limitless when we live in purpose. Studies continue to show that having a purpose in life leads to a longer, healthier, wealthier life. Y'all, this is the bag we need to strive to get. Whatever is important to you is the fuel that feeds your soul. It is imperative that we explore and experience all that we have been given. So, if there is even an inkling of feeling or thought that you are supposed to do something other than what you are doing, then you need to make the shift to purpose living. God makes no mistakes. He is intentional and instructional. He has placed a blessing on every life that he has created, and therefore living in purpose is the call for every individual.

Practicing purpose is like life-giving oxygen, and you must choose to breathe it. When you practice something, you get good at it. And when you are good at anything, it will lead you to a healthy, vibrant and dynamic life . That is the epitome of practicing purpose.

Sis, I am cheering you on. I want you to do your best and live your best, because you are worth it! We have to embrace our experiences because every one of them that we encounter ultimately leads us to our purpose. Purpose is the light of your life story, and you are the only human being that has the ability to tell it well.

May you sizzle, sparkle, and shine as you choose to live the life you were born for!

REFERENCES

INTRODUCTION
Genesis 1:26-27 (ESV)

Chapter 1 – It Happened to Me

"Our experience is the catalyst for shaping the best version of ourselves."

Definition: Experience, "the fact or state of having been affected by or gained knowledge through direct observation or participation" https://www.merriam-webster.com/dictionary/experience.

Quote: "Don't waste anything." – Julie Landi

Scripture: Philippians 4:8 (ESV)

Definition: Paradigm Shift, "an important change that happens when the usual way of thinking about or doing something is replaced by a new and different way." https://www.merriam-webster.com/dictionary/paradigm%20shift

Chapter 2 – The Power of Choice

"Life is like a box of chocolates." – Forrest Gump

Communication skills you need:

https://www.skillsyouneed.com/ips/communication-skills.html

Chapter 3 – Unblock Me

"We are becoming who we have chosen to be."

Scripture: John 16:33 (ESV)

Chapter 4 – Self-Soul Care

"Bask in the warmth of your own light." –Amy Perez

Helpful Links:

- https://www.gotquestions.org/soul-care.html
- https://www.huffpost.com/entry/12-exercises-for-the-soul_b_10242238

Chapter 5 – Hope Heals

- "I feel that my story is my legacy and I have to pass it on." – Tina Turner

Root word for healing and its definition:
https://www.ncbi.nlm.nih.gov/pmc/articles/PMC4653605/#:~:text=The%20word%20healing%20comes%20from,wholeness%20or%20achievement%20of%20cohesion

Scripture: 2 Corinthians 12:10 (ESV)

Chapter 6 - Forgiveness

"Declutter the dust from your soul."

Scriptures:

- Galatians 6:7 (ESV)
- John 10:10 (ESV)

Reference:
https://www.psychologytoday.com/us/basics/forgiveness#:~:text=Forgiveness%20is%20the%20release%20of,those%20who%20have%20been%20victimized

Chapter 7 – Understanding Your Worth

"Fitting in is not an option, but being yourself is."

Scripture: Genesis 1:26-27 (ESV)

Reference: Rachel Hollis, *Girl, Stop Apologizing*

Chapter 8 – The Remarkable You

Embrace the flashlight of your soul

Seasons of life: https://www.livescience.com/25202-seasons.html

Fall, Winter, Spring, Summer: https://learning-center.homesciencetools.com/article/winter-science-lesson

Chapter 9 – No Regrets

"Be in this choice, this life, this now, and stop imagining that reality could be or could have been anything other than what it is." – Nancy Colier

"12 things people regret the most before they die" by Loly Daskal:

https://www.lollydaskal.com/leadership/12-things-people-regret-the-most-before-they-die/

Brain research regarding regret:
https://www.nature.com/articles/nn1514

Chapter 10 – Own Your Life

"Love yourself first and everything else falls in line. You really have to love yourself to get anything done in this world." – Lucille Ball

Chapter 11 – Rhythm and Stride

"Not even me can stop me." – Jennifer Lewis

Chapter 12 – Practice Purpose

"Live the life you were born for."

Scripture: James 1:5 (ESV)

The stages of a woman's life:
https://www.nuffieldhealth.com/article/womens-life-stages

Multitasking: https://ascellus.com/how-cbt-can-help-with-multitasking/#:~:text=Multitasking%20and%20the%20brain&text=Studies%20have%20also%20shown%20that,regulation%20of%20motivation%20and%20emotion.

For more information regarding the studies on the benefits of purpose living:
www.psychologytoday.com/us/blog/the-main-ingredient/202002/why-do-you-need-purpose-in-life

www.ingramcontent.com/pod-product-compliance
Lightning Source LLC
Chambersburg PA
CBHW070425230125
20710CB00012B/453